ON THE COVER
Shinumo Camp, Grand Canyon National Park, Arizona
Photography by: NPS/Melissa Trammell

Preserving Natural Resources in the National Parks
Fiscal Year 2010 Report to Congress

Natural Resource Report NPS/NRSS/NRR—2011/456

National Park Service
Natural Resource Stewardship and Science
Office of Education and Outreach
1201 Oakridge Drive, Suite 150
Fort Collins, CO 80525

October 2011

U.S. Department of the Interior
National Park Service
Natural Resource Stewardship and Science
Fort Collins, Colorado

The National Park Service, Natural Resource Stewardship and Science office in Fort Collins, Colorado publishes a range of reports that address natural resource topics of interest and applicability to a broad audience in the National Park Service and others in natural resource management, including scientists, conservation and environmental constituencies, and the public.

The Natural Resource Report Series is used to disseminate high-priority, current natural resource management information with managerial application. The series targets a general, diverse audience, and may contain NPS policy considerations or address sensitive issues of management applicability.

All manuscripts in the series receive the appropriate level of peer review to ensure that the information is scientifically credible, technically accurate, appropriately written for the intended audience, and designed and published in a professional manner.

Views, statements, findings, conclusions, recommendations, and data in this report do not necessarily reflect views and policies of the National Park Service, U.S. Department of the Interior. Mention of trade names or commercial products does not constitute endorsement or recommendation for use by the U.S. Government.

This report is available on the Natural Resource Publications Management Web site (http://www.nature.nps.gov/publications/nrpm/) on the Internet.

Please cite this publication as:

National Park Service. 2011. Preserving natural resources in the national parks: Fiscal year 2010 report to Congress. Natural Resource Report NPS/NRSS/NRR—2011/456. National Park Service, Fort Collins, Colorado.

NPS 909/111147, October 2011

Contents

Creating Stewards of Our Natural Resources 1

Chapter 1: Natural Resources in the National Parks 3
Reporting and Measuring Progress 3

Chapter 2: Natural Resource Programs in the National Park Service 7
Park and Regional Natural Resource Programs 7
Network Programs 7
   Cooperative Ecosystem Studies Units 7
   Exotic Plant Management Teams 9
   Inventory and Monitoring Networks 10
   Research Learning Centers 13
Servicewide Natural Resource Programs 13
   Air Quality Program 14
   Biological Resource Management Program 14
   Geologic Resources Program 16
   Water Resources Program 17
   Environmental Quality Program 18
   Natural Sounds Program 19
   Social Science Program 19
   Climate Change Response Program 20
   Resource Protection Program 21
   Natural Resource Preservation Program 21

Chapter 3: Accomplishments by Region 25
Alaska Region 25
Intermountain Region 29
Midwest Region 33
National Capital Region 36
Northeast Region 39
Pacific West Region 43
Southeast Region 48

Chapter 4: Servicewide Accomplishments 53

Appendixes
A Natural Resource Challenge Funding in Parks 57
B Natural Resource Program Funding–Servicewide Programs 58
C Biological Resource Management Competitive Projects 63
D Water Resource Program Projects 64
E Climate Change Response Program Projects 68
F Resource Protection Projects 72
G Natural Resource Preservation Program Projects 73
H Park-Oriented Biological Support Projects 83

Indexes
Park Index 84
State and Territory Index 87

Creating Stewards of Our Natural Resources

The National Park Service manages some of North America's most intact ecosystems. America's parks are oases of biodiversity as much as they are breathtaking landscapes for the vacationing public. Parks serve as refuges for sensitive species and provide important habitat to keep common species thriving. They act as classrooms that demonstrate the complexities of nature, places to observe the effects of climate change in a natural laboratory setting and showcase how science is being used to support ecosystem adaptation.

Emerging issues have challenged us to find new ways to conserve our park resources. We are now thinking and acting at the landscape scale assisted by unprecedented partnerships with other land managers and increasing engagement of citizens in science. By enlisting the public in our stewardship mission through programs like the BioBlitz, the National Park Service brings students and volunteers of all ages to parks to work side-by-side with scientists. For example, volunteers form the core of monitoring and invasive species removal programs at many sites, and student fellowships and programs provide opportunities for young people to make significant contributions to the knowledge of natural resources, such as the discovery of a saber tooth cat fossil at Badlands National Park by a seven-year-old Junior Ranger.

To address current and future challenges, National Park Service professionals continue to rely upon science. It is the compass that guides our management actions and illuminates complex issues—whether protecting the sounds of nature at the Grand Canyon, restoring natural processes in the Florida Everglades, or studying retreating glaciers in the Rocky Mountains. We also place a high importance on communicating our vision, actions, and discoveries to local and national audiences.

As we face the future, I believe that national parks will become increasingly critical to the preservation and stewardship of our national natural heritage. National Park Service employees are dedicated to educating the next generation of park stewards, increasing relevancy of protected areas, and winning advocates for the parks while achieving our science and resource management goals. While highly dedicated, National Park Service staff cannot preserve these special places alone—we need the support of the American public. Because of the Natural Resource Challenge, the National Park Service is in a better position to protect our natural heritage and address emerging issues; however, there is still much work to do.

I am honored to lead the employees of the National Park Service. We have one of the most skilled and passionate workforces in the country. We have many challenges ahead, but I am confident that we will meet them with the same excellence we demonstrated over this past year.

Jonathan B. Jarvis

Jonathan B. Jarvis
Director
National Park Service

Volunteers planting along Roaches Run Wildlife Sanctuary, Virginia, part of the George Washington Memorial Parkway. NPS photo.

Chapter 1: Natural Resources in the National Parks

For nearly 100 years, since the passage of the Organic Act in 1916, the National Park Service has endeavored to protect many of America's most scenic and ecologically diverse lands. *The Natural Resource Challenge: The National Park Service Action Plan for Preserving Natural Resources* ("the Challenge") was launched in 1999 to assist this effort by improving our knowledge of natural resources in parks.

More than ten years later, the National Park Service has made significant progress in addressing the three major challenges outlined in the plan:

- protecting native species and their habitats
- providing leadership for a healthy environment
- connecting parks to protected areas and parks to people

Reporting and Measuring Progress

When the Challenge was first funded in FY 2000, Congress requested that the National Park Service report on Challenge-related expenditures and accomplishments. This report responds to that request and offers a summary of the state of natural resources across the National Park System in FY 2010 by providing financial details and accomplishments for Servicewide natural resource stewardship programs funded by the Challenge as well as other sources. Table 1-1 compares FY 2010 natural resource stewardship funding to FY 1999 levels, before the Challenge was initiated.

To measure the effectiveness of its natural resource programs, the National Park Service uses the performance goals outlined in the Department of the Interior's *GPRA Strategic Plan: Fiscal Year 2007–2012*, which was established in accordance with the Government Performance and Results Act (GPRA) of 1993. Table 1-2 lists strategic plan targets, FY 2010 results, and Servicewide natural resource programs supporting park performance. The table compares FY 2010 actual performance to projected planned performance as set forth in the National Park Service's FY 2011 budget justification for all GPRA goals reported to Congress.

Piping plover chick waiting to be banded and weighed at Apostle Islands National Lakeshore, Wisconsin. NPS photo by Ted Gostomski.

Table 1-1. Comparison of Natural Resource Stewardship Program funding in the National Park Service in FY 1999 (prior to the Natural Resource Challenge) and FY 2010

Program components	Funding (thousands of dollars)		
	FY 1999	FY 2010	Change
Natural Resource Challenge–affected programs			
Air Quality Program	6,285	8,884	2,599
Biological Resource Management Program	0	9,969	9,969
Cooperative Ecosystem Studies Units[a]	0	125	125
Geologic Resources Program	1,918	3,420	1,502
Inventory and Monitoring Program	5,787	45,495	39,708
Natural Resource Data and Information Program	1,424	1,955	531
Natural Resource Preservation Program	5,432	8,099	2,667
Research Learning Centers (20 centers total, 12 funded by the Challenge)[b]	0		
Resource Damage Assessment and Restoration Program	873	1,453	580
Resource Protection Fund	0	283	283
Water Resources Program	4,754	13,870	9,116
SUBTOTAL – Natural Resource Challenge-affected programs	26,473	93,553	67,080
Programs not affected by Natural Resource Challenge			
Climate Change Response Program[c]	0	10,000	10,000
Everglades—Comprehensive Restoration Plan (CERP)	0	4,789	4,789
Everglades—Critical Ecosystem Studies Initiative	12,000	3,873	-8,127
Everglades Task Force Support	800	1,320	520
Glen Canyon Adaptive Management Program	0	96	96
Natural Sounds Program (formerly Overflight Program)	200	3,565	3,365
Social Science Program[d]	850	1,769	919
SUBTOTAL – Non-Natural Resource Challenge programs	13,850	25,412	11,562
SUBTOTAL – SERVICEWIDE NATURAL RESOURCE PROGRAMS	40,323	118,965	78,642
NATURAL RESOURCE STEWARDSHIP PROGRAMS IN NPS UNITS, OTHER FIELD UNITS, AND SERVICEWIDE NATURAL RESOURCE SUPPORT PROGRAMS	66,708	119,443	52,735
TOTAL NATURAL RESOURCE STEWARDSHIP	$107,031	$238,408	$131,377

[a] Total reflects program funding after transfers to parks or regions.
[b] Total reflects funding after transfers to 12 Challenge-funded Research Learning Centers in FY 2001 ($898,000) and FY 2002 ($1,800,000). The remaining eight centers are funded by park base and partner funds.
[c] The Climate Change Response Program (initially called the Global Climate Change Program) was first funded in FY 2010.
[d] Total includes Public Use Statistics funding ($264,000).

Table 1-2. NPS Strategic Plan targets and results for FY 2010

Goals related to strategies to restore, maintain, sustain, and protect resources	Servicewide natural resource program supporting park performance
BUR Ia3A Visibility: Visibility in 95% of NPS reporting parks has remained stable or improved. Actual: 97% (158 of 163 parks). (**exceeded**)	Air Quality
BUR Ia3B Ozone: Ozone in 87% of NPS reporting parks has remained stable or improved. Actual: 100% (159 of 159 parks). (**exceeded**)	
BUR Ia3C Atmospheric Deposition: Atmospheric deposition in 77% of NPS reporting parks has remained stable or improved. Actual: 93% (52 of 56 parks) remained stable or improved. (**exceeded**)	
BUR Ia1B Invasive Plants: 0.82% (13,231 of 1,611,867) of acres infested with invasive plants being maintained as free of invasive plants and 2.5% of acres (41,033.5 of 1,611,867) treated. Actual: 1.08% (17,353.7) of acres controlled and 4.6% (74,577.4 acres) of acres treated. (**exceeded**)	Biological Resources Management
BUR Ia2A Threatened and Endangered Species: 34.7% (343 of 986) of federally listed species in parks making progress toward recovery. Actual: 34.4% (339). (**failed**)[a]	
BUR Ia2B Species of Management Concern: 13.3% (680 of 5,115) of park populations of native species of management concern are managed to desired condition. Actual: 13.5% (688). (**exceeded**)	
BUR Ia2C Invasive Animals: 13.05% (116 of 889) of park populations of exotic (i.e., non-native) invasive animal species are effectively controlled. Actual: 12.82% (114). (**failed**)[b]	
BUR Ia1A Disturbed Lands Restoration: 4.78% (12,237 of 255,827) of disturbed parkland acres targeted in a park plan for restoration have been treated for restoration. Actual: 5.62% (14,385 of 255,827 (**exceeded**)	Geologic Resources
BUR Ia9 Paleontological Sites: 45.1% (1,900 of 4,210) of paleontological localities in good condition. Actual: 52.8% (2,223 of 4,210). (**exceeded**)	
BUR Ia4A Water Quality Miles: 99.1% (166,000 of 167,500) of surface water stream miles in parks meet state and federal water quality standards as defined by the Clean Water Act. Actual: 99.2% (166,200 of 167,500). (**exceeded**)	Water Resources
BUR Ia4B Water Quality Acres: 79% (3,466,900 of 4,388,500) of surface water acres in parks meet state and federal water quality standards as defined by the Clean Water Act. Actual: 79% (3,466,800 of 4,388,500). (**met**)	

Sources: *Budget Justifications and Performance Information Fiscal Year 2011* and NPS Office of Strategic Planning
[a] During the past decade, the status of those species listed as "unknown" in NPS units have been determined, and recovered species such as the bald eagle have been removed from federal listing. Making progress toward the recovery of more than one-third of listed species in parks will require additional resources above current levels of dedicated effort.
[b] The National Park Service considers the goal effectively met. Five parks failed to meet effectively controlled status for eight populations of invasive animals. Three parks exceeded their target goal. The reasons for failing to meet the target varied, including that populations have exceeded the ability of the parks to effectively control populations in the near future.

Chapter 2: Natural Resource Programs in the National Park Service

The natural resource program in the National Park Service operates on park, regional, network, and Servicewide levels. The Challenge improved the capacity of programs at every level to deal with complex issues that affect our ability to preserve natural resources in units of the National Park System. This chapter describes those programs and their brief FY 2010 accomplishments. More detailed accomplishments representative of the many natural resource activities across the National Park System can be found in Chapters 3 and 4.

Note: Within this chapter, names of programs are followed by an abbreviation, which will be used to indicate program leads for the accomplishments listed in the following chapters.

Upper Columbia Basin Network aquatic biologist preparing water quality monitoring equipment in Craters of the Moon National Monument and Preserve, Idaho. NPS photo by Paulina Tobar-Starkey.

Park and Regional Natural Resource Programs

Natural resource programs in parks are integral to the NPS effort to preserve resources. The Challenge provided base increases to 36 parks to be used for basic natural resource capability in small parks, invasive species control, threatened and endangered species recovery, and native species management. These parks continue to benefit from Challenge funding today with an increased capacity for dealing with threats to natural resources (see Appendix A for natural resource funding in parks receiving Challenge increases). Regional programs also benefited from the Challenge through the establishment of specialist positions with focused knowledge and skills, such as aquatic resource professionals, that assist multiple parks with natural resource management issues.

Funding from the Challenge remains today, although some parks and regions report that these funds have eroded as fixed costs such as salaries rise. This leaves less money to fund both natural resource projects and park-based positions created by the Challenge. To help compensate, parks leverage Challenge funding through partnerships and project funding such as the Natural Resource Preservation Program (page 21). All regions report that competition for this project funding has increased. In FY 2010 Servicewide cost of living increases helped take some pressure off regional offices and park units.

Network Programs

Increasingly complex natural resource issues require park managers to obtain a broad-based understanding of the status and trends in natural resource condition, work with other agencies, and communicate with the public. In recognition of this, the Challenge funded four programs that organize parks into biogeographic networks across the country: Cooperative Ecosystem Studies Units, Exotic Plant Management Teams, Inventory and Monitoring Networks, and Research Learning Centers. These network programs allow parks to accomplish much more together than they could individually—and the networks save valuable money by consolidating staffs, programs, and projects and leveraging limited funding with partners. The networks work closely with park, regional, and national natural resource programs; federal and state agencies; universities; nonprofit organizations; and other partners to accomplish shared resource protection goals.

Cooperative Ecosystem Studies Units (CESU)

Cooperative Ecosystem Studies Units are multi-agency partnerships between universities, federal agencies, and other institutions. The National Park Service is one of 13 federal agencies within the CESU network, which was established in FY 1999 with leadership from the National Park Service, U.S. Geological Survey, and other federal agencies. In FY 2010 a total of 210 universities (including 44 minor-

Revegetation plot at Pipe Spring National Monument, Arizona, part of a vegetation management project through the Colorado Plateau CESU. NPS photo.

The "biological crossroads" of the Niobrara River valley, Nebraska, where Great Plains CESU cooperators performed a Natural Resource Condition Assessment in 2010. NPS photo.

ity institutions) and 54 nonfederal research partners participated in the CESU network. Participation in CESUs enables the National Park Service to obtain high-quality science, usable knowledge for resource managers, responsive technical assistance, continuing education, and cost-effective research programs.

CESUs operate within all regions of the National Park Service. Since FY 2001 Challenge funding, allocated through base transfers to regions, has supported NPS participation in 12 CESUs. In FY 2010 three additional CESUs—the North and West Alaska CESU, Great Rivers CESU, and Californian CESU—received funding. The funds are used to station a coordinator at the host university. Host universities provide office space and administrative support to the coordinators and access to university faculty, students, staff, and resources. NPS coordinators work with NPS park and program managers to identify research, technical assistance, and education needs and to provide specialized expertise and assistance available from the universities and federal agency partners. Remaining funds support research, technical assistance, and educational activities, as well as operating expenses. In FY 2010 NPS coordinators were duty stationed at 15 CESU host universities.

An equal level of funding ($154,920) is allocated to each of the 12 CESUs supported by the Challenge; the rest of the funding ($125,960) provided administrative support and coordination activities at the NPS and Department of the Interior (DOI) levels. The three newly funded CESUs received $154,000 each. In FY 2010 CESUs facilitated 836 projects across the country and supported a diverse range of funding sources that totaled nearly $46 million (Table 2-1). Since FY 2001 the CESU network has initiated 6,458 projects totaling more than $314 million (Table 2-2).

Major themes within the CESU network in FY 2010 include:

- **Changes in Funding:** In FY 2010 some CESUs reported a level or declining trend due to reductions in matching state funds, new non-CESU cooperative agreements, and other factors. Others reported a substantial increase in project numbers and project dollars.
- **Student Involvement:** Undergraduate and graduate students participate in projects, internships, fellowships, and student career positions, offering much-needed experience for future researchers.
- **Opportunities for Inter-agency and Inter-university Projects:** As the CESUs mature, opportunities for inter-agency and inter-university projects are increasing, including those that involve ecosystem-level research such as a remote sensing project for vegetation at **Catoctin Mountain Park (MD), Harpers Ferry Park (MD, WV), Prince William Forest Park (VA)**, and Dyke Marsh Wildlife Preserve (managed by **George Washington Memorial Parkway [MD, VA]**).
- **Climate Change Projects:** Climate change is an increasingly important focus area for CESUs, and cross-boundary collaboration and data-sharing are particularly critical. The CESUs, Research Learning Centers, and Inventory and Monitoring Networks organized joint meetings and workshops, with emphasis on climate change issues. CESU coordinators serve as experts on regional and national committees associated with climate change response and adaptation and work with the new Landscape Conservation Cooperatives in cooperation with the U.S. Fish and Wildlife Service (USFWS) and other DOI bureaus.
- **Focus on Diversity:** CESUs continue to further diversity opportunities through projects such as a Native American internship program with the resource management staff at **Yellowstone National Park (ID, MT, WY)** facilitated by the Rocky Mountains CESU.
- **Varied Duties for Research Coordinators:** CESU research coordinators performed important collateral duties in 2010, organizing and conducting workshops, symposia, regional summits, and training sessions on natural and cultural research and management issues.

Table 2-1. Project activity and funding by region and individual Cooperative Ecosystem Studies Unit (CESU), FY 2010

Region	CESU	Partners[a]	Projects	Funding ($)
Alaska	North and West Alaska[b]	19	38	2,271,270
Intermountain	Colorado Plateau	29	139	5,215,694
	Desert Southwest	23	53	2,152,136
	Rocky Mountains	21	172	10,796,168
Midwest	Great Lakes-Northern Forest	39	18	3,163,493
	Great Plains	25	37	338,093
	Great Rivers[b]	27	16	1,718,926
National Capital	Chesapeake Watershed	31	43	2,204,239
Northeast	North Atlantic Coast	18	25	1,288,716
Pacific West	Californian[b]	29	36	2,033,415
	Great Basin	21	32	1,685,671
	Hawaii-Pacific Islands[b]	18	30	1,773,722
	Pacific Northwest	28	80	4,007,852
Southeast	Gulf Coast	36	33	1,332,647
	Piedmont-South Atlantic Coast[b]	29	24	1,236,057
	South Florida/Caribbean	19	38	3,613,492
	Southern Appalachian Mountains	22	22	995,908
TOTAL			836	$45,827,499

[a]Because some agencies partner with more than one CESU, the total would equal more than the total listed in the text.
[b]These CESUs were not funded by the Natural Resource Challenge.

Table 2-2. Cooperative Ecosystems Studies Unit (CESU) projects and funding, FY 2001–FY 2010

Fiscal year	CESUs in network	Projects initiated	Total funding ($)
2001	8	260	10 million
2002	12	380	15 million
2003	16	540	19 million
2004	17	650	27 million
2005	17	635	32 million
2006	17	728	39 million
2007	17	848	43 million
2008	17	777	45 million
2009	17	804	38 million
2010	17	836	46 million
TOTAL		6,458	$314 million

Exotic Plant Management Teams (EPMT)

Native communities of plants and animals across the National Park System are threatened by invasive plant species. EPMTs were established to respond to the expanding invasive plant problem across the country. They contribute to invasive plant control goals Servicewide by working closely with other NPS programs and through cooperation and collaboration with other agencies, tribal nations, state parks, and private landowners. This collaborative effort has increased the areas under invasive plant management.

EPMTs participate in all aspects of invasive plant management including prevention, inventory, monitoring, and treatment. Sixteen teams serve more than 220 parks across the country, providing a framework and first response to exotic plant invasions. The teams are headquartered in a region or park unit and operate over a wide geographic area. Staffed

Mapping invasive species in Alaska. NPS photo.

Idaho's Craters of the Moon National Monument and Preserve and Upper Columbia Basin Network staff sampling macroinvertebrates in water holes in the monument's lava fields. NPS photo.

by highly trained individuals with expertise in plant identification, plant ecology, invasive plant management, and pesticide use, the teams have emerged as local and regional invasive plant experts.

In FY 2010 EPMTs inventoried 488,475 acres within parks and 16,492,063 acres of non-park lands in cooperation with other federal and state agencies. Within park lands, 92,631 acres infested with invasive plants were newly mapped and more than 250 species on 13,596 acres were treated during the year. The Alaska EPMT used American Recovery and Reinvestment Act (ARRA) funds to double its capacity, facilitating inventories of new areas and implementation of an early detection and rapid response strategy for Alaska. Youth programs continue to play an important role in EPMTs, with several former program participants now in permanent positions. A program review was initiated in summer 2010 to assess the effectiveness of the EPMT program, now almost 10 years old, in meeting the goals and needs of managing invasive plants in national parks.

Inventory and Monitoring Networks (I&M)

The Inventory and Monitoring Program is an essential part of the National Park Service's effort to revitalize the natural resource program and to improve park management through greater reliance on scientific information. Thirty-two bioregional networks, which share core funding and professional staff, include 270 parks with significant natural resources. By leveraging limited funding and staffing through partnerships and linking to park management and planning, the I&M networks provide scientifically sound, organized, and retrievable information about natural resources to support management decision making, park planning, research, education, and public understanding. For most parks, the I&M Program provides the primary means of measuring the status and trends in the condition of park resources.

The I&M Program provides funding, technical assistance, and coordination for parks to complete 12 basic natural resource inventories and to monitor the condition, or "health," of park natural resources based on key vital signs. The basic natural resource inventories assess and document the current condition and knowledge of natural resources in parks and establish a solid baseline for long-term monitoring plans. The investigations increase our knowledge and understanding about park resources, including many new and exciting insights, and provide information to address a wide variety of resource management issues and activities. In FY 2010 the I&M Program completed an additional 91 data sets for a total of 2,545 data sets developed and delivered to parks (Table 2-3). At current funding levels, the delivery of all 2,767 data sets to the 270 I&M parks will require at least another five years.

Vital signs monitoring tracks a subset of physical, chemical, and biological elements and processes of park ecosystems that are selected to represent the overall health or condition of park resources, known or hypothesized effects of stressors, or elements that have important human values. As of September 2010, all 270 I&M parks (100 percent) had identified their vital signs, developed a state-of-the-art monitoring plan, and implemented operational monitoring of priority resources. All 270 I&M parks can now provide "current condition" estimates for key measurements of the condition of high-priority natural resources (Table 2-4). While funding restrictions limit initial monitoring to the highest priority vital signs or those that are already funded by another source, parks expand monitoring efforts by augmenting Challenge funds with personnel and funding from other sources, establishing partnerships, and monitoring several vital signs and parameters together. The number of networks and parks that expect to monitor a vital sign in various categories with currently available funding is summarized in Table 2-5.

To manage relevant natural resource data collected by NPS staff, cooperators, researchers, and others, the I&M Program is integrating five separate data systems into the Integrated Resource Management Applications (IRMA) data system. This system, based on DOI and industry standards and best practices, will allow data exchange and integration among different data systems within and external to DOI agencies.

Inventory and monitoring results are used in Natural Resource Condition Assessments and park planning documents (Table 2-4) and are provided to managers, planners, interpreters, scientists, and the general public. Combined with an effective education program, inventory and monitoring results can contribute not only to solving park issues but also to larger quality-of-life issues that affect surrounding communities and to the environmental health of the nation. As a direct result of Challenge funding, the I&M Program has become a significant component of the overall scientific and information management infrastructure and expertise of the National Park Service.

Table 2-3. Number of Inventory and Monitoring Program parks, out of the total 270 parks in the program, that received the minimal set of inventory products identified in 1992, FY 2001–FY 2010

Inventory	Fiscal year									
	2001	2002	2003	2004	2005	2006	2007	2008	2009	2010
Natural resource bibliography	257	263	270	270	270	270	270	270	270	270
Base cartography data	248	260	270	270	270	270	270	270	270	270
Air quality data	250	250	250	270	270	270	270	270	270	270
Air quality related values	0	0	0	48	100	150	175	210	240	270
Climate inventory	0	197	270	270	270	270	270	270	270	270
Geologic resources inventory	2	14	17	52	68	92	117	138	164	184
Soil resources inventory	37	57	57	59	70	100	141	171	190	207
Water body classification	0	220	270	270	270	270	270	270	270	270
Baseline water quality data	225	270	270	270	270	270	270	270	270	270
Vegetation inventory	22	27	36	51	62	80	127	155	173	197
Species lists	210	270	270	270	270	270	270	270	270	270
Species status/distribution	0	0	0	3	44	100	200	270	270	270
TOTAL	1,251	1,828	1,982	2,103	2,234	2,412	2,650	2,834	2,927	3,018
Completed before 2001	473	473	473	473	473	473	473	473	473	473
GPRA Actual	778	1,355	1,509	1,630	1,761	1,939	2,177	2,361	2,455	2,545
GPRA Target	768	1,121	1,498	1,637	1,771	1,942	2,145	2,338	2,450	2,767
Percent GPRA Complete[a]			54.5	58.9	63.6	70.1	78.7	85.3	88.7	92

[a]Percent GPRA complete values are based on the baseline of 2,767 total data sets to be delivered to the 270 I&M parks during the initial phase of natural resource inventory development.

Table 2-4. Annual accomplishments of the 270 Inventory and Monitoring Program parks in completing the planning and design of their long-term monitoring programs and implementing operational monitoring of vital signs, FY 2006–FY 2010, and projected completion, FY 2011–FY 2012. Data and expertise provided by the I&M networks are a key source of data for park Natural Resource Condition Assessments, Resource Stewardship Strategies, and other park planning and management efforts.

	Actual and projected accomplishments for vital signs monitoring and resource assessments	Number of parks completed by end of fiscal year					Number of parks projected	
		2006	2007	2008	2009	2010	2011	2012
Planning and design phase	Identify and synthesize existing information	270	270	270	270	270	270	270
	Prioritize and select vital signs	250	270	270	270	270	270	270
	Monitoring plan completed, peer-reviewed, and approved—operational monitoring begun	157	197	253	270	270	270	270
	"Current condition" values available for specific vital signs—operational monitoring ongoing	104	157	197	253	270	270	270
Monitoring and assessments completed	Park Natural Resource Condition Assessments Completed	0	0	1	8	13	26	40
	Park Resource Stewardship Strategy plans completed that incorporate results from vital signs monitoring and Natural Resource Condition Assessments	0	1	1	3	5	13	13

Table 2-5. Number of parks in the Inventory and Monitoring Program that will monitor each vital sign category using existing funding (including partnerships with others where the networks will deliver data summaries to park managers and planners). Vital signs that will be monitored in fewer than 30 parks are not listed.

Vital sign category	Example measures (varies by network)	Number of parks
Weather and climate	Temperature, precipitation, wind speed, ice on/off	246
Water chemistry	pH, temperature, dissolved oxygen, conductivity	211
Land cover and use	Area in each land cover and use type; patch size and pattern	203
Invasive/exotic plants	Early detection, presence/absence, area	200
Birds	Species composition, distribution, abundance	189
Surface water dynamics	Discharge/flow rates (cfs), gauge/stage height, lake elevation, spring/seep volume, sea level rise	158
Ozone	Ozone concentration, damage to sensitive vegetation	140
Wet and dry deposition	Wet deposition chemistry, sulfur dioxide concentrations	114
Visibility and particulate matter	IMPROVE network; visibility and fine particles	113
Fire and fuel dynamics	Long-term trend of fire frequency, average fire size, average burn severity, total area affected by fire	105
Vegetation complexes	Plant community diversity, relative species/guild abundance, structure/age class, incidence of disease	101
Mammals	Species composition, distribution, abundance	93
Forest/woodland communities	Community diversity, coverage and abundance, condition and vigor classes, regeneration	93
Soil function and dynamics	Soil nutrients, cover and composition of biological soil crust communities, soil aggregate stability	91
Stream/river channel characteristics	Channel width, depth, and gradient; sinuosity; channel cross-section; pool frequency and depth; particle size	89
Aquatic macroinvertebrates	Species composition and abundance	86
Threatened and endangered species and communities	Population estimates, distribution, sex and age ratios	85
Air contaminants	Concentrations of SOCs, PCBs, DDT, Hg	71
Groundwater dynamics	Flow rate, depth to groundwater, withdrawal rates, recharge rates, volume in aquifer	69
Amphibians and reptiles	Species distribution and abundance, population age/size structure, species diversity, percent area occupied	54
Grassland/herb communities	Composition, structure, abundance, changes in treeline	51
Fishes	Community composition, abundance, distribution, age classes, occupancy, invasive species	50
Insect pests	Extent of insect-related mortality, distribution and extent of standing dead/stressed/diseased trees, early detection	50
Riparian communities	Species composition and percent cover, distribution and density of selected plants, canopy height	45
Nutrient dynamics	Nitrate, ammonia, DON, nitrite, orthophosphate, total K	45
Primary production	Normalized differential vegetation index (NDVI), change in length of growing season, carbon fixation	41
Wetland communities	Species composition and percent cover, distribution and density of selected plants, canopy height, aerial extent	40
Microorganisms	Fecal coliform, *E. coli*, cyanobacteria	30
Water toxics	Organic and inorganic toxics, heavy metals	30
Invasive/exotic animals	Invasive species present, distribution, vegetation types invaded, early detection at invasion points	29
Coastal/oceanographic features and processes	Rate of shoreline change, sea surface elevations, area and degree of subsidence through relative elevation data	29

Climate change ambassadors survey for mountain goats in Glacier National Park, Montana, as part of a joint program between the Southern California and Crown of the Continent Research Learning Centers. NPS photo.

Research Learning Centers (RLC)
Beginning in FY 2001 the National Park Service created 20 Research Learning Centers to foster new and cutting-edge knowledge about park resources through research, education, and public engagement. Challenge funding supports 12 RLCs; eight RLCs are funded through partner support and existing park base funds. Centers are typically park-based but generally provide research and educational services to a network of parks.

The mission of the RLCs is to increase the effectiveness of both research and communication of science results in the national parks by

- facilitating the use of parks for scientific inquiry,
- supporting science-informed decision making,
- communicating the relevance of and providing access to research knowledge, and
- promoting resource stewardship through partnerships.

Partnerships are the key to RLC success. RLCs engage hundreds of park partners including universities; schools; non-profit organizations; community groups; federal, state, and tribal agencies; and NPS programs. They implemented and pioneered multiple citizen science programs, including BioBlitzes and longer-term programs to monitor the health of a species or ecosystem. RLC programs can quickly adapt to unforeseen park information needs via an adaptable and skilled professional staff and numerous partnerships. RLC support is an integral component of successful resource management, interpretation, and I&M programs at many parks.

In FY 2010 RLC research coordinators helped establish and implement more than 1,000 research projects through collaboration with researchers; many of these projects directly informed park management decisions. Cumulative RLC efforts helped produce more than 100 peer-reviewed journal articles and involved more than 450 university students in park research. Many RLCs offer internship and/or fellowship programs that target high-priority NPS research, science education, and science communication needs. Efforts to communicate science included on-line multimedia products, publications, and exhibits; workshops and seminars on topics such as invasive species, mercury, and wildlife conservation; and hands-on science activities.

Climate change continues to be a focal point for RLCs. Because they are at the nexus of research, education, and outreach programs, RLCs foster collaboration and partnerships to increase parks' capacity to assess resource conditions and vulnerabilities to climate change. RLCs increase the National Park Service's ability to plan for and adapt to climate change at the local, regional, and landscape scales; implement appropriate responses; and assist with internal and external communication of climate change issues.

Servicewide Natural Resource Programs
Servicewide natural resource programs provide invaluable services to the nearly 400 units of the National Park Service. Within each discipline, program staff offer policy and regulatory expertise, provide technical assistance and advice, help develop plans and proposals, and guide education and outreach efforts. The Challenge enhanced these Servicewide efforts by strengthening four basic program areas:

- Air Quality
- Biological Resource Management
- Geologic Resources
- Water Resources

National Park Service natural resource management includes a number of other programs outside of the Challenge that provide Servicewide leadership in specialized areas:

- Environmental Quality
- Natural Sounds
- Social Sciences
- Climate Change Response

The efforts of these Servicewide programs, as well as park and regional programs, are supported by two natural resource funding sources. The Resource Protection Program offers project funding for resources at risk. Natural Resource Preservation Program funding allows parks to undertake natural resource management projects beyond the scope of park budgets. Total FY 2010 funding for Servicewide natural resource programs and funding sources is included in Appendix B.

Air quality web cam site.

Monitoring of mercury in wet deposition in Acadia National Park, Maine. NPS photo by Colleen Flanagan.

Air Quality Program (AQ)

The Air Quality Program is responsible for preserving, protecting, and enhancing air quality and air quality–related values in the National Park System in accordance with the NPS Organic Act and the Clean Air Act. Working in regulatory and policy arenas to accomplish this goal, the Air Quality Program emphasizes the collection and analysis of credible air quality information to support scientifically sound resource management decisions in parks and pursues collaborative efforts with regulators, the scientific community, and other stakeholders to improve air quality in parks. The Air Quality Program has four main focus areas:

- **Collaboration**: The program engages with states, the U.S. Environmental Protection Agency (EPA), and other stakeholders to help protect park resources from the adverse effects of air pollution by developing appropriate air policies and strategies. In FY 2010 division staff reviewed 17 state regional haze plans in an effort to reduce visibility-impairing pollutants and improve visibility. Staff also reviewed 15 new source permit applications for proposed projects near NPS units, conducted independent air quality impact assessments, and suggested better pollution control technology to minimize emissions.
- **Interpretation and Outreach**: To promote public knowledge of air quality conditions and effects in NPS areas, the program hosts the Air Quality Web Camera Network, in which 16 cameras at 15 parks show the visible effects of air pollution. Associated Web pages (www.nature.nps.gov/air/WebCams/) display air quality and weather information. The staff assists parks with ozone and fine particle health advisory programs, which alert visitors and employees when concentrations have the potential to reach unhealthy levels.
- **Monitoring**: Monitoring activities identify the status and trends of ambient air quality conditions in NPS units, provide air quality assessments, and respond to park-specific monitoring issues. The data are also used in support of special studies and other research. In cooperation with partners, the program operates at least five different networks of ambient air quality monitoring sites in NPS units, measuring more than 10 different parameters including ambient gases, meteorology, deposition chemistry, particulate matter, and visibility. FY 2010 accomplishments include measuring ozone with portable systems in 14 parks as part of the I&M Program, measuring roadside nitrogen oxides in winter in **Yellowstone National Park (ID, MT, WY)** to determine the air quality impacts of over-snow vehicles for winter use planning and modeling of possible use scenarios, and participating in a collaborative monitoring and modeling program to study the effects of oil and gas development on local air quality in Colorado, Wyoming, and Utah.
- **Ecosystem Effects**: The program has identified natural resources sensitive to air pollutants in more than 200 parks, as well as specific ecosystem indicators that respond to pollution and the thresholds associated with a given response. This information can be used to establish park management goals, report and communicate on resource trends and condition, and ultimately help protect sensitive resources in parks. FY 2010 projects included monitoring air quality in the Southeast Alaska Network to assess the extent to which cruise ship emissions and other sources are linked to enhanced pollutant deposition and ecological effects and assessing the impact of mercury bioaccumulation on bats and insects in **Mammoth Cave National Park (KY)** and other Cumberland/Piedmont Network park units.

Biological Resource Management Program (BRM)

The Biological Resource Management Program provides professional, science-based support to protect, preserve, and manage biological resources and related ecosystem processes in the National Park System. In addition to supporting Exotic Plant Management Teams, the Biological Resource Management Program focuses its efforts in nine areas:

- **Ecosystem Restoration and Management**: The program provides coordination and technical support for restoration work in parks including, in FY 2010, **War in the Pacific National Historical Park (Guam), Bandelier National Monument (NM), Grand Teton National Park (WY),** and multiple prairie parks. Staff also consulted

Recording biological soil crust abundance and diversity as part of the Sonoran Desert Network's vegetation classification plot surveys. NPS photo.

on contaminants issues in **Indiana Dunes National Lakeshore (IN)** and **Saratoga National Historical Park (NY)**.
- **Human Dimensions of Biological Resource Management**: Staff provide expertise in applied social science to improve stakeholder engagement and public participation, strategic communication, recreation and biological resource management, and citizen science and stewardship. In FY 2010 they partnered in a multi-disciplinary initiative to advance social science contributions to climate change response planning, initiated investigations into the human dimensions associated with reducing the impacts of lead from hunting and fishing activities on public lands, and assisted with **Yellowstone National Park (ID, MT, WY)** winter use planning.
- **Integrated Pest Management**: The program reduces risk from pests and pest-related management activities affecting the public, employees, and park resources. In FY 2010 staff coordinated with the NPS Public Health Program to provide policy interpretation and technical guidance regarding management of tick-borne disease and Africanized honey bees; facilitated a pilot turf stewardship project in the Midwest Region; and initiated a water features project to assess intake and discharge of water used in NPS fountains, monuments, etc., to promote pollution prevention and address new EPA discharge legislation. Staff reviewed and approved 2,610 individual pesticide use proposals.
- **Invasive Species**: The Invasive Species Program addresses an ever-increasing threat from invasive species. Projects emphasized preventing the introduction and spread of invasive species through monitoring and cleaning boats infested with aquatic invasive species such as quagga mussels; confining potential forest insects and diseases in firewood; using weed-free products to prevent exotic plant introduction; and developing collaborative monitoring, treatment, and management strategies with adjacent landowners and agencies.
- **Landscape Ecology and Conservation**: The program contributes to the conservation of wildlife migration routes, dispersal corridors, and other important habitats needed to allow native wildlife to move. Movement is necessary to meet daily and seasonal needs, maintain viability and biodiversity in response to climate change, and persist in fragmented landscapes. In FY 2010 program staff worked to strengthen continental conservation efforts through increased awareness, interaction, and collaboration with state, tribal, and local governments; federal and international agencies; and the public.
- **Threatened and Endangered Species**: Staff work to restore and stabilize threatened and endangered (T&E) species listed under the Endangered Species Act and the habitats upon which they depend. In FY 2010 staff coordinated three climate change response projects, prepared and presented outreach materials for the **Biscayne National Park (FL)** BioBlitz, established an NPS special collection with the American Museum of Natural History, and led the DOI Bison Conservation Initiative.
- **Vegetation Inventory**: Program staff develop vegetation inventory products such as taxonomic classification, vegetation keys, digital maps and associated databases, and project reports for the 270 I&M parks to fill resource assessment, park management, and conservation needs. As of FY 2010 the program had completed inventories for 35 percent of the parks and had ongoing projects in 150 parks. (The 35 percent completion figure includes final reviewed and web-mounted products for 91 parks. The 197 GPRA complete vegetation inventories in Table 2-3 represent draft maps delivered to parks.)
- **Wildlife Health**: This program provides professional veterinary and wildlife management support on the policy and technical aspects of wildlife diseases and their management, preventive health actions, fertility control, field anesthesia, and animal welfare issues. In FY 2010 staff led implementation of the inaugural NPS Institutional Animal Care and Use Committee, collaborated with the NPS Office of Public Health to implement a One Health approach to health management, provided guidance on emerging wildlife diseases such as white-nose syndrome in bats, and conducted research furthering understanding of chronic wasting disease in elk.
- **Wildlife Management**: Staff coordinate wildlife management efforts to assure policy compliance and continuity, ensure

Preparing to plug the first of 39 wells in Big South Fork National River and Recreation Area, Tennessee and Kentucky, using American Recovery and Reinvestment Act funds. NPS photo.

Geologic resources scoping meeting at Lewis and Clark National Historical Park, Oregon and Washington. NPS photo.

that management efforts are technically adequate and scientifically credible, and act as principal technical advisor for activities relating to Servicewide management of wildlife and wildlife habitats. In FY 2010 staff established a five-year cooperative agreement with the Wildlife Conservation Society for multi-park wolverine, migratory bird, and bison conservation projects and initiated a Servicewide review of ungulate management in cooperation with park and regional offices.

Biological Resource Management competitive funds are used to address resource management issues concerning ecosystems, ecosystem process, wildlife, and vegetation throughout the National Park System. In FY 2010 20 projects were funded for a total of $531,500 (Appendix C).

Geologic Resources Program (GR)

The Geologic Resources Program provides leadership and guidance for the protection and management of the geologic and interdependent ecosystem resources of the National Park System. The program carries out an array of activities under six categories:

- **Geologic Features, Landscapes, and Processes**: This program assists parks with paleontological resources, cave and karst resources, coastal geology, geologic mapping, soil resources, and active geological processes. In FY 2010 staff worked with partners and contractors to complete four new paleontological resource reports encompassing 37 parks. Staff developed several cave and karst management plans, made recommendations for structure relocation or removal at cave parks, reviewed cave and karst resource protection programs, and led the federal partnership with the National Cave and Karst Research Institute. Staff spearheaded NPS involvement in the development of DOI regulations governing the management and protection of paleontological resources on federal lands. Staff completed digital geologic maps for 20 parks, held scoping meetings for mapping needs and geologic resource management issues at 18 parks, completed geologic reports for 21 parks, and finalized soil resource inventories for 11 parks with the Natural Resources Conservation Service and National Cooperative Soil Survey. Coastal geology staff advised parks on hurricane and storm impacts, restoration, and coastal resource inventory and monitoring and provided Servicewide support on climate change topics such as sea level rise and coastal adaptation.
- **Energy and Mineral Development**: Staff provide NPS managers with assistance in addressing energy and mineral development issues inside and adjacent to park boundaries through expertise in mining, petroleum geology and engineering, regulations, policy, reclamation, and impact mitigation. In FY 2010 staff addressed park protection concerns regarding conventional and renewable energy development outside park boundaries and assisted more than 65 parks in six regions with energy- and mineral-related issues. At present, more than 200 parks could be impacted by conventional and renewable energy development outside park boundaries; 30 parks contain nearly 680 active private mineral or oil and gas operations within their boundaries. To improve the effectiveness of the regulations, staff initiated a rulemaking to update and revise the NPS regulations governing the exercise of nonfederal oil and gas rights in parks (36 CFR Part 9, Subpart B).
- **Restoration—Disturbed Lands and Abandoned Mineral Lands**: Staff prepare technical guidance, review park work plans for technical adequacy, and oversee the NRPP–Disturbed Lands Restoration fund source (page 22). Staff also oversee, coordinate, and support land restoration and human safety hazard mitigation at abandoned mineral land (AML) sites in parks. In FY 2010 the program obligated $24.57 million in ARRA funds for 49 projects addressing hazardous or environmentally detrimental conditions at 923 AML features in 31 NPS units in 15 states.
- **Geologic Resource Information**: Staff provide geosciences data and policy input to planning documents and nonfederal oil and gas planning efforts in parks and offer resource-specific technical assistance and data and technical reviews of park planning documents. In FY 2010 staff reviewed planning documents and commented on an environmental impact statement (EIS) for nonfederal oil and gas development at **Big**

South Fork National River and Recreation Area (KY, TN), general management plan at Golden Gate National Recreation Area (CA), shoreline management plan at Indiana Dunes National Lakeshore (IN), NPS Impairment Guidance, and Director's Order-12 *National Environmental Impact Handbook*.

- Climate Change Impacts and Vulnerabilities: The program helps parks face the challenge of managing resources with respect to climate change—for example, rates of shoreline erosion in parks are increasing as sea level rises, storms intensify, and storm surges reach further inland. In FY 2010 staff coordinated a storm hazard project and completed storm vulnerability assessments at Kaloko-Honokohau National Historical Park and Pu'ukohola Heiau National Historic Site (HI) and George Washington Birthplace National Monument (VA).
- Active Geological Processes and Hazards: Staff help parks assess and evaluate active geological processes such as erosion, landslides, rock falls, and tsunamis; protect park visitors and infrastructure from the effects of these processes; and assist in developing restoration plans for lands disturbed by the effects of these processes and climate change. In FY 2010 staff provided incident-related technical assistance for 10 projects in 10 parks across five NPS regions. Staff also provided parks with policy and permitting assistance in response to a number of proposed actions that could impact processes in park coastal waters.

Water Resources Program (WR)

The Water Resources Program provides leadership for the preservation, protection, and management of the water and aquatic resources in NPS units. Water resource issues include policy, planning, and regulatory review; water quality; water rights; floodplain management; erosion and sediment control; fisheries management; protection of wetland and riparian habitats; and ocean and coastal resources. In FY 2010 the Water Resources Program continued oversight and implementation of four Challenge programs in addition to the newly funded Ocean and Coastal Resources Program.

- Aquatic Resource Professionals: Fourteen field-based aquatic resource professional positions were funded in 2010, with vacant positions being filled at Jean Lafitte National Historical Park (LA) and Chattanooga, Tennessee. The National Capital Region position remains vacant. These specialists provide park managers with the expertise to address high-priority aquatic resource needs.
- Natural Resource Condition Assessments: Natural Resource Condition Assessments develop science-based information for park-level resource planning, decision making, and partnership activities. Each assessment synthesizes existing scientific data from a variety of sources to report on current conditions (and trends where possible), critical data gaps, and

Upper Twin Lakes, Lake Clark National Park and Preserve, Alaska. NPS photo by Dan Young.

Long-term water quality monitoring conducted in Ofu Lagoon in National Park of American Samoa. NPS photo by Anne Farahi.

Restoration of grounding site at Biscayne National Park, Florida, in February 2011. Large holes in the sandy-bottom seagrass habitat were filled to allow recovery of flora and fauna. NPS photo by Amanda Bourque.

resource condition influences for a subset of important park natural resources. As of September 2010, assessment projects and final reports had been completed for 12 NPS units with at least 13 additional park reports scheduled for completion in 2011.

- **Water Quality Monitoring**: Vital signs water quality monitoring protocols are in place, and water quality monitoring is being conducted in all 32 I&M networks (Appendix B). The Water Resources Program continues to assist with the data management components of network water quality monitoring.
- **Water Resource Protection Projects**: The Water Rights Branch supported park water resource protection projects in FY 2010 to collect water resource data to meet data reporting obligations, develop predictive capabilities through surface or groundwater models, monitor impacts of reservoir releases on riparian/wetland vegetation and of groundwater development on endangered fish, and investigate the importance of fresh and brackish water on anchialine ponds (landlocked ponds with an underground connection to the ocean). More than $650,000 supported these activities and assistance from the Office of the Solicitor in various legal forums to secure and protect water resources.
- **Ocean and Coastal Resources**: The Ocean and Coastal Resources Program was funded for the first time in FY 2010. The program adopted strategies from the 2006 *Ocean Park Stewardship Action Plan* and regional strategic implementation plans for ocean and coastal park stewardship. Ocean and coastal resource technical specialists work in three regions, and marine pollution and marine fisheries specialists work at the Servicewide level. In FY 2010 funds were distributed through the competitive Servicewide Comprehensive Call to projects that strengthen the science-based foundation for managing and conserving ocean and coastal resources and help park managers better understand ocean and coastal ecosystems and the human roles in them.

See Appendix D for a list of FY 2010 Water Resources Program projects.

Environmental Quality Program (EQ)

This program serves a key role in ensuring that the National Park Service meets the requirements of the 1916 Organic Act and makes informed decisions that maintain the unspoiled beauty, rich landscapes, and abundant resources of our parks. It helps the National Park Service accomplish its mission through several functions: environmental planning and compliance, resource protection, and external reviews. Many of the projects under this program are multi-year efforts that involve other agencies at the federal and state levels.

- **Resource Protection**: This program provides technical assistance, training, case management, and restoration project management to help parks address incident-caused injuries to resources. Under the Park System Resources Protection Act (16 U.S.C. 19jj); Oil Pollution Act; and Comprehensive Environmental Response, Compensation, and Liability Act (CERCLA), the National Park Service is authorized to take actions to prevent or minimize injuries, assess and seek recovery of compensatory damages, and restore injured resources associated with discharges of oil, releases of hazardous substances, and other incidents. In FY 2010 the Resource Protection program was involved with the Deepwater Horizon Oil Spill, both facilitating cost documentation and reimbursement efforts for spill response and leading Servicewide efforts for damage assessment and early restoration scoping processes. Staff managed 40 damage assessment cases, facilitated 20 quick-claim settlements for restoration, and initiated the Grand Ditch Breach restoration plan/EIS for **Rocky Mountain National Park (CO)**, with a draft plan expected in fall 2011. In FY 2010 monies from settlements deposited in DOI's Natural Resources Damage Assessment and Restoration (NRDAR) Fund totaled $4.4 million, and funds withdrawn from the NRDAR Fund for restoration totaled $1.75 million.
- **Environmental Planning and Compliance**: This program provides policy development, technical assistance, training, and project management to parks in the areas of impact analysis and conservation planning under the National Environmental Policy Act (NEPA) and related statutes. Program staff assist parks with complex, controversial, and potentially precedent-setting NEPA analyses and decisions and provide assistance that is generally not available

Setting up sound monitoring equipment at Everglades National Park, Florida. NPS photo.

at the park or regional levels. In FY 2010 the program managed more than $4 million of environmental planning work in 25 parks. Projects supported include the South Florida and Caribbean Parks exotic plant management plan/EIS, the **Cape Cod National Seashore (MA)** Herring River restoration plan/EIS, the **Hawaii Volcanoes National Park (HI)** plan/EIS for protecting and restoring native ecosystems by managing non-native ungulates, and **Yellowstone National Park (WY, MT, ID)** winter use planning.

- **External Review**: This program is the focal point for NPS external environmental reviews. Program staff operate, manage, review, and track environmental documents having shared interests or concerns. Staff distribute non-NPS documents to appropriate NPS professionals for their review and comment on the potential impacts of applicants' proposals on NPS resources and values and coordinate and consolidate NPS comments into a single response. These external reviews help applicants avoid or mitigate impacts to NPS resources and values as well as to NPS programs administered under statutory or administrative authorities. Staff are also a source of information pertaining to significant environmental developments that may affect NPS resources. In FY 2010 the program managed approximately 1,500 external reviews.

Natural Sounds Program (NSP)

The Natural Sounds Program, established in 2000, protects, maintains, and restores soundscape resources and values by working in partnership with parks and others to increase scientific and public understanding of the value and character of park soundscapes. The program continues to expand capacity and productivity through its work with diverse governmental, non-profit, and academic partners.

An important element of the program's mission involves working with the Federal Aviation Administration (FAA) to implement the National Parks Air Tour Management Act. Staff monitor acoustic conditions, collect and analyze data, develop ambient acoustic baseline information, and provide planning assistance, including drafting and reviewing park plans and NEPA documents. Staff started new air tour management plans at **Petrified Forest National Park (AZ)** and **Golden Gate National Recreation Area, Muir Woods National Monument, Point Reyes National Seashore,** and **San Francisco Maritime National Historical Park (CA)** and conducted acoustical monitoring at 11 NPS sites in preparation for upcoming plans.

To help address emerging issues such as cultural and historic soundscapes, noise impacts underwater, and impacts from energy development projects near parks and from species adapting to changes in climate by moving in and out of historic niches, staff assisted more than 76 parks with 126 soundscape-related projects. Staff completed acoustic monitoring at 23 units and analyzed data for and wrote 11 acoustic reports, which help further the science of acoustics in protected areas and NPS understanding of the overall role that acoustics play in ecosystem health and visitor enjoyment. Staff trained employees at five parks and initiated the process for assessing noise source issues (e.g., energy development, watercraft, ORVs, construction equipment, motorcycles).

To increase awareness of the importance of natural soundscapes in parks, staff produce educational and outreach products. Staff completed a handbook to help park staff discuss soundscape issues with visitors, revised and distributed program brochures, and developed a soundscape module as part of a training course for the Arthur Carhart National Wilderness Training Center.

Social Science Program (SS)

The Social Science Program conducts and facilitates research that provides public input into park planning and management, investigates economic interactions between parks and nearby communities, and develops methods and techniques to improve the management of visitor use. The National Park Service uses this information to improve visitor services, enhance civic engagement, protect natural and cultural resources, and manage parks more effectively. Staff focus their efforts in the following areas:

- **Comprehensive Survey**: The periodic Comprehensive Survey of the American Public provides key insights into public opinions, knowledge, and behavior regarding parks. Comparison of the first survey

published in 2001 with a second survey conducted in 2009 will provide relevant insights for park management. The results of the second survey are expected in 2011.
- Money Generation Model: The model estimates the economic impact of park visitation on surrounding communities and economies in terms of employment and sales. These quantifiable measures of the economic benefits of park visitation can be used in planning, concessions management, budget justifications, policy analysis, and marketing. The *Economic Benefits to Local Communities from National Park Visitation and Payroll, 2009* report, which contains the latest estimates, indicates that park visitation supported 247,000 jobs nationally and generated more than $9 billion in labor income.
- Public Use Statistics: The Public Use Statistics Office coordinates visitor counting protocols Servicewide and provides visitation statistics and forecasts for parks and other units administered by the National Park Service. The *Statistical Abstract 2009* report indicates a total of more than 285 million recreation visits System-wide.
- Technical Assistance: Staff work with parks, regions, and program offices to obtain Office of Management and Budget approval for surveys of visitors and the public under the Paperwork Reduction Act. In FY 2010 23 surveys were approved by the Office of Management and Budget.
- Visitor Services Project: The Visitor Services Project conducts customized, park-specific studies of visitors—who they are, what they do, and what their opinions are. Park managers use these data to improve operations, protect resources, and better serve the public. In FY 2010 the program conducted 17 studies in 16 parks.
- Visitor Survey Card: The Visitor Survey Card project measures visitor satisfaction at more than 310 NPS units and gathers data concerning visitor understanding of a park's national significance. It is the primary source of data used to measure the GPRA goals of visitor satisfaction (goal IIa1A) and visitor understanding (goal IIb1). During FY 2010 the overall level of visitor satisfaction was 97 percent, including 92 percent for park facilities, 95 percent for visitor services, and 95 percent for recreational opportunities.

Climate Change Response Program (CCRP)

The Climate Change Response Program was established in 2008 to facilitate Servicewide communication and provide scientific expertise, guidance, and information that support NPS actions to protect natural and cultural resources and facilities from the detrimental impacts of rapid climate change. The program involves parks, regions, and national program offices as well as external partners, including universities, non-profit organizations, and other federal agencies. The program plays an

Visitors at Zion National Park, Utah. Photo by the National Park Service Visitor Services Project/ Gail Vander Stoep.

The *Climate Change Response Strategy*, released in 2010.

important role in the DOI's climate change initiative and received funding in FY 2010 to support three interrelated efforts:

- Enhance monitoring that leverages existing I&M networks and promotes new partnerships for effective decision making
- Develop adaptation planning and response strategies for promoting ecosystem resilience, preserving cultural heritage, and protecting facilities and infrastructure
- Provide a core level of subject matter expertise and technical assistance to enable parks to implement priority short-term adaptation actions and plan for long-term effects (areas of expertise include climate change science, communication, resource management, wildlife, monitoring, planning, coastal hazards, cultural anthropology, and energy efficiency)

In undertaking these efforts, the National Park Service is collaborating with other DOI bureaus by providing personnel and project support for the emerging Landscape Conservation Cooperatives and Climate Science Centers. The program has taken a role as co-lead of the Great Northern Landscape Conservation Cooperative and has committed funding to positions in three additional Landscape Conservation Cooperatives (South Atlantic, North Atlantic, and Pacific Islands) and two Climate Science Centers (Northwest and Alaska). In addition, the program has funded an urban landscape adaptation coordinator through the National Capitol Region. The program contributes to the department's high priority performance goal of identifying the areas and species ranges in the United States that are most vulnerable to climate change and implementing comprehensive climate change adaptation actions in these areas.

In FY 2010 the program funded more than $2.7 million in climate change projects, many of which help parks understand resource vulnerability. Funded projects were located in every NPS region and include natural resource, cultural resource, and interpretation and education projects. See Appendix E for a list of projects.

Resource Protection Program (RP)

The Resource Protection Program supports projects that propose innovative approaches involving natural resource specialists, protection rangers, researchers, and partners from other agencies to focus on resources at risk. In FY 2010 the Resource Protection Program distributed $283,000 for such projects. A list of Resource Protection projects active in FY 2010 is included in Appendix F.

Natural Resource Preservation Program (NRPP)

The NRPP provides funding to parks for natural resource management projects beyond the scope of park budgets. The NRPP supports diverse activities in areas such as wildlife, fisheries, and vegetation management; specialized inventories; planning; mitigation actions; and restoration activities.

Challenge funding has had a significant impact on the program. Funding increased from $5,432,000 in FY 2000 to $12,693,000 in FY 2003. Budget cuts, however, decreased NRPP funding: since 2003, the NRPP has lost $4,594,000. These reductions translate into fewer on-the-ground projects in parks per year and reduced performance outcomes.

Despite this, the NRPP continues to serve as a comprehensive, accountable funding source for resource management projects. Pre-panel technical reviews, professional cost estimates, and Servicewide Comprehensive Call (SCC) guidance continue to increase the accountability and efficiency of this funding source. Nearly half of NRPP funds are available for general park-level natural resource management projects; the balance targets specific needs such as small park projects, disturbed lands restoration, threatened and endangered species, and funds that are distributed to the regions for their use for natural resource projects in parks (Table 2-7). Lists of NRPP projects funded in FY 2010 are included in Appendix G.

Alaska Special Projects (NRPP–AK) funding was established to allow the National Park Service to undertake projects that improve the protection and management of NPS units in Alaska, which are managed under the Alaska National Interest Lands Conservation Act and other Alaska-specific requirements. Funding focuses on the highest priority natural resource projects that lack adequate funding from other sources. As competition for other NRPP fund sources increases, more reliance

Planting endangered sentry milk-vetch (*Astragalus cremnophylax* var. *cremnophylax*) at Grand Canyon National Park, Arizona. NPS photo.

Swift fox (*Vulpes velox*) captured and released at Badlands National Park, South Dakota. NPS photo.

is being placed on Alaska Special Projects funding. FY 2010 projects included studies to quantify the thickness of the Harding Icefield; assess the status of peregrine falcons, Dall's sheep, trumpeter swans, and wolves; monitor subsistence fisheries; and more.

Disturbed Lands Restoration (NRPP–DLR) provides funding for parks to restore disturbed lands—lands where natural conditions and processes have been degraded, damaged, or destroyed by development (e.g., facilities, roads, mines, dams) and/or by agricultural practices. The land disturbances and human safety hazards at abandoned mineral land (AML) sites continued to be major issues on NPS lands; approximately 2,600 AML sites with 9,100 individual features are known to exist in 127 units of the National Park System. Restoration assists in the recovery of these disturbed areas through direct manipulation of degraded ecosystem components. In FY 2010 the DLR program funded 12 projects in 16 parks in four NPS regions. Seven DLR projects were completed in 11 parks, resulting in the restoration of approximately 237 acres of severely disturbed land in a wide variety of environmental settings.

Natural Resource Management (NRPP–NRM) projects make up the largest segment of the NRPP. Projects eligible for funding through this source include resource management actions; tactical biological studies; development of new physical science theory, management approaches, and protocols; and combined research and follow-up resource management or mitigation actions. In FY 2010 funding was distributed to 35 projects.

NRPP funding is provided to regions to distribute between Regional Program Block Allocation and Regional Small Park Block Allocation projects. These sources fund important projects that would generally have a difficult time finding funding elsewhere due to their small scale. Regional reports emphasize the importance and value of these fund sources for allowing smaller park units to meet basic natural resource needs without having to compete against larger, well-staffed parks. **Regional Program Block Allocation (NRPP–RB)** projects improve natural resource knowledge and condition, including projects such as specialized inventories currently outside the scope of the Servicewide I&M Program and mitigation actions (e.g., fossil inventories and invasive plant or invasive animal control). In FY 2010 Regional Program Block Allocation funding was allocated to 63 projects in 47 parks (Table 2-8).

The **Regional Small Park Block Allocation (NRPP–SP)** helps small parks achieve their natural resource goals by funding projects for parks that fall in the lower third of funding for all parks. In FY 2010 the program funded 51 projects in 45 parks (Table 2-9).

Servicewide (NRPP–SW) projects address the needs of Servicewide programs (e.g., Air Quality, Water Resources, etc.) that are not met within the budgets of the programs. Some projects are designed to provide tools or capacity that will benefit many NPS programs, while others respond to issues that are beyond the capacity of the base programs to fund. These special projects are often interdisciplinary in nature and may include activities with professional organizations, publications, or Servicewide databases. In FY 2010 Servicewide funding supported 22 projects, including an energy strategy session, a risk assessment and action plan for aquatic and marine invasive species, and the 2010 BioBlitz at Biscayne National Park (FL).

Threatened and Endangered Species (NRPP–T&E) projects are on-the-ground conservation efforts that contribute to the long-term goal of the NPS Threatened and Endangered Species Program to increase the number of park populations of listed species that are making progress toward recovery and to restore these species when they have been extirpated from parks. FY 2010 fully funded projects addressed endangered species in Great Smoky Mountain National Park (NC, TN), Padre Island National Seashore (TX), and Saint Croix National Scenic Riverway (MN, WI).

The NPS Natural Resource Preservation Program and the U.S. Geological Survey–Biological Resources Discipline jointly fund USGS biological projects that provide exploratory research and technical assistance for parks. In FY 2010 the National Park Service contributed $236,000 and the USGS Biological Resources Discipline contributed $387,201 for these **Park-Oriented Biological Support (POBS)** projects. In addition, both bureaus added a portion of their climate change funding to fund an additional four POBS projects ($83,803 in NPS climate change funds and $83,804 in USGS climate change funds). Information about the projects active in FY 2010 is found in Appendix H.

Table 2-7. Natural Resource Preservation Program (NRPP) project totals and funding by category, FY 2010

NRPP funding categories	Number of projects	FY 2010 funding ($)
Alaska Special Projects	11	467,000
Disturbed Lands Restoration	12	790,000
Natural Resource Management	35	3,139,000
Regional Program Block Allocation	63	1,303,000
Regional Small Park Block Allocation	51	933,000
Servicewide Projects[a]	22	764,000
Threatened and Endangered Species	13	467,000
Park-Oriented Biological Support[b]	16	236,000
TOTAL	227	$8,099,000

[a]At the end of FY 2010, an $18,200 difference existed between authorized and actual obligated NRPP Servicewide funds.
[b]The Climate Change Response Program funded four additional Park-Oriented Biological Support projects.

Table 2-8. Natural Resource Preservation Program–Regional Program Block Allocation projects by region, FY 2010

Region	Number of parks	Number of projects	Funding ($)
Alaska	2	9	187,000
Intermountain	6	6	186,000
Midwest	11	12	186,000
National Capital	5	10	186,000
Northeast	9	10	186,000
Pacific West	6	8	186,000
Southeast	8	8	186,000
TOTAL	47	63	$1,303,000

Table 2-9. Natural Resource Preservation Program–Regional Small Park Block Allocation projects by region, FY 2010

Region	Number of parks	Number of projects	Funding ($)
Alaska	2	2	19,000
Intermountain	13	13	242,000
Midwest	9	11	170,000
National Capital	3	3	19,000
Northeast	5	6	116,000
Pacific West	6	8	161,000
Southeast	7	8	206,000
Total	45	51	$933,000

Chapter 3: Accomplishments by Region

Seven regions encompass the nearly 400 diverse units of the National Park System. These regions face many of the same broad-scale issues, such as invasive species, energy development, and climate change. Each region, however, contains unique natural resources that are affected by these issues in different ways, posing challenges specific to that region. Park, regional, network, and Servicewide staff work together with partners, cooperators, and volunteers to address these issues. This chapter details some of the significant FY 2010 natural resource accomplishments within each region.

Alaska Region (AKR)

Alaska is expansive and diverse, with climate and topography that constitute a virtual subcontinent. The state's NPS units protect representative natural, cultural, and historic features of this immense landscape. Ten were created by the 1980 Alaska National Interest Lands Conservation Act.

To address new and increasing challenges in the 21st century, the Alaska Region produced a natural resource strategic plan, which was finalized in February 2011. Ten focus areas encompass the range of issues fundamental to Alaska's national parks and provide a framework for effective natural resource management over the next 10 years. The focus areas include the condition of park natural resources, backcountry and wilderness areas, ocean and coastal resources, climate change response, collaborative conservation, visitor use, harvest of natural resources, living laboratories, information management, and fostering professionalism. Parks accomplished projects addressing all these areas in FY 2010.

Park Accomplishments

Cape Krusenstern National Monument, Kobuk Valley National Park, Noatak National Preserve: Primary users of these NPS units, all located north of the Arctic Circle, are local Inupiat residents who retain subsistence rights to maintain traditional lifestyles. University of Alaska–Fairbanks cooperators developed a narrative bibliography based on historical themes of significance, providing a reference for the region's history and resources for use by managers, planners, cultural resource specialists, and the public. The bibliography will assist in managing consumptive uses of subsistence resources, such as hunting and gathering and traditional access. (CESU)

Denali National Park and Preserve: Researchers are performing targeted habitat assessments of the globally rare arboreal lichen

USGS graduate student measuring stream discharge, Emerson Creek, Lake Clark National Park and Preserve, Alaska. NPS photo by Dan Young.

Eriodema pedicellatum in the park. Field work, including installation of more than 40 permanent plots, was completed in FY 2010, and data analysis will continue in FY 2011. Based on current data, researchers believe that the southern part of the park may represent the largest known population of this species on the planet, which is significant because it is extirpated or declining in all other parts of its known geographic range. (NRPP–AK)

Denali and Central Alaska Network staff completed the twenty-third consecutive year of monitoring the occupancy of nesting territories and reproductive success of golden eagles (*Aquila chrysaetos*) in the park. In 2010 occupancy remained stable, while nesting success and fledgling production were similar to the last several years. The Denali golden eagle study is the only contemporary study of the nesting ecology of this species in northwestern North America. The results of this long-term monitoring program are becoming more important on a continental scale as issues concerning the management and conservation of this species increase. (I&M)

Gates of the Arctic National Park and Preserve, Wrangell-St. Elias National Park and Preserve: A study is underway to test distance-sampling techniques to estimate park-wide abundance of Dall's sheep (*Ovis dalli*), a species of interest, in six of Alaska's largest NPS units. One of the most readily viewed large mammals, Dall's sheep may serve as indicators of climate and vegetation change. In FY 2010 pilot-observer teams flew 152 hours in Gates of the Arctic and 70 hours in the northern portion of Wrangell-St. Elias. Data analysis will produce abundance estimates in those areas. The data will be used to understand population trends, focus management actions, and identify hypotheses for further evaluation. (NRPP–AK)

Glacier Bay National Park and Preserve: Park managers are assessing the impacts of increasing cruise ship traffic on endangered humpback whales (*Megaptera novaeangliae*). Observers on cruise ships document the frequency and severity of encounters between ships and whales; data analysis will continue into 2011. Outcomes to date include a protocol for communicating real-time information on the location of severe encounters (near misses) between whales and ships, which allows resource management to implement actions, including slowing ship speed, in areas where these severe encounters are occurring. (NRPP–NRM)

Katmai National Park and Preserve: Park staff launched a study to determine whether current management actions are sustaining healthy brown bear (*Ursus arctos*) populations in the preserve. In FY 2009 researchers flew

Ewes and rams photographed during the 2010 aerial survey of Dall's sheep in Gates of the Arctic National Park and Preserve, Alaska. NPS photo by Stacia Backensto.

Mine closure efforts in the Alaska Region. Installation of a bar gate in Kenai Fjords National Park, Alaska. NPS photo by Fritz Klasner.

Completed mine closure in Wrangell-St. Elias National Park and Preserve, Alaska. NPS photo.

aerial surveys to determine population density of the bears. They located 105 brown bear groups, with 194 bears. Initial analysis shows that while harvest has increased, the rate of harvest appears to be in the range of what is generally acceptable for brown bear populations. The demographic data do not indicate problems with population health. (BRM)

Kenai Fjords National Park: To help maintain the scenic and environmental integrity of the Harding Icefield and its outflowing glaciers by increasing understanding of those resources, staff initiated a project to quantify the thickness of the icefield. Researchers developed a method for measuring ice thickness using ground penetrating radar; this technology will have applications in other NPS units in Alaska. Maximum ice depths recorded were 400–600 meters; additional measurements will be taken. Project results will allow researchers to model future landscapes in anticipation of glacial retreat due to climate change and hazard analysis near the glacier terminus. (CESU, NRPP–AK)

Klondike Gold Rush National Historical Park: In cooperation with the U.S. Forest Service (USFS), the Southeast Alaska Network completed a lichen inventory at the park, identifying at least 766 species. In an area of only 13,000 acres, this finding represents one of the largest numbers of lichens per unit area ever reported and the largest number of lichen species reported from any U.S. national park. The study yielded at least 75 species previously unknown to science—nearly 10 percent of all species observed—and the first Northern Hemisphere member of the genus *Steinera*, otherwise known only from Antarctica and New Zealand. (I&M)

Lake Clark National Park and Preserve: The park, through a CESU agreement with the University of Alaska Environment and Natural Resources Institute, began a three-year project to study marine nutrients in wolf (*Canis lupis*) diet across Alaska. Preliminary results indicate that at least half of Lake Clark's wolf packs make extensive use of salmon during late summer and into early winter. (CESU)

Wrangell-St. Elias National Park and Preserve: Eight abandoned and potentially hazardous mine openings were closed in Wrangell-St. Elias, along with one in **Denali National Park and Preserve** and five in **Kenai Fjords National Park**. Several sites were at mines eligible for listing on the National Register of Historic Places, which required extra care to preserve the mines' cultural resources while closing access to dangerous underground workings. The 14 closures, funded in part by ARRA and State of Alaska funds, represent twice as many closures in the region as in any prior year.

Yukon-Charley Rivers National Park and Preserve: Alaska contains some of the most important rocks on Earth for studying dinosaurs of the Cretaceous period, the last days of the dinosaurs. Researchers are in the midst of a two-year project to study these rocks along the Yukon River and associated drainages. FY 2010 field work yielded fossils ranging from rich beds of Permian brachiopods to Pleistocene mammoth tracks. Some of the project's findings will result in the revision of the geologic maps of the preserve. The project will continue into FY 2011. (NRPP–AK)

Yukon-Charley saw the first statistically significant increase in the moose (*Alces alces*) population since 1987, with an estimate of 1,331 individuals based on aerial surveys. The density of moose was calculated as 0.43 moose per square mile, with an unusually high number of yearlings indicating exceptionally good production and/or survival of 2008 calves. (I&M)

Regional Projects

Alaska Park Science: Twice a year *Alaska Park Science* reports information from the physical, biological, cultural, and social sciences; history; and related humanities in Alaskan national parks. In FY 2010 the region published two new issues focusing on the Arctic/Beringia International Symposium and the I&M Program in Alaska and launched a new website for the journal (www.nps.gov/akso/nature/science/ak_park_science/). In addition, a FY 2010 review of the journal's effectiveness by a panel of NPS science education, interpretation, and communication professionals indicates it is widely read, appreciated, and used by NPS readers and others within and outside Alaska. (NRPP–RB)

Climate Change Scenario Planning: The National Park Service began a three-year climate

Coastline of Kenai Fjords National Park, Alaska. USGS photo by Tjibbe Stelwagen.

change scenario planning project in Alaska to help park managers, employees, cooperators, and others understand climate trends; anticipate future changes that may affect resources, assets, and operations in parks and surrounding areas; and identify a range of possible climate change response strategies. Thirty-two participants representing a range of NPS and other agency stakeholders in Alaska (USFWS, USFS, Bureau of Land Management [BLM], and the National Oceanic and Atmospheric Administration [NOAA]) participated in webinars and a training workshop in August 2010. Initial scenarios will inform a series of I&M network–based workshops in 2011 and 2012. (CCRP)

Digital Shoreline Maps: Coastal parks in Alaska lack an accurate, standardized digital marine shoreline referenced to a local tidal stage or a vertical tidal datum shoreline referenced to mean high water. Park boundaries in Alaska are generally based on mean high water or mean lower low water. The lack of a consistent tidal datum reference in the National Hydrographic Dataset, the recognized source for hydrographic data, results in incorrectly delineated NPS legal borders. A professionally defensible shoreline dataset for 10 Alaska coastal parks will be used by resource management, collaborators, and the public through the USGS's National Map Program. (WR)

Oceanographic Data Made Available: The Southeast Alaska Network recently completed the evaluation and re-processing of a large legacy data set on the physical oceanography of Glacier Bay. Dating to 1993, the data were previously of uncertain quality and not easily accessible. Now park staff, partners, and researchers can query and download portions of or the entire dataset from the network's website. These data represent the longest-running and most intact oceanographic dataset from the waters of Southeast Alaska. (I&M)

Social Science Strategy: Park representatives gathered for a workshop to begin implementation of a regional social science strategy. The purpose of this workshop was to discuss the role of indicators and standards in managing recreational use in parks, introduce the idea of a regional program of indicator and standard development, and identify a list of visitor use–related indicators that are common across the Alaska Region. The final product from this workshop was a regional research proposal from social scientists at the University of Vermont and Utah State University to build a program of research to develop specific measurable indicators, measurement protocols, and associated standards that arise from the broad categories identified in the workshop. (NRPP–SP)

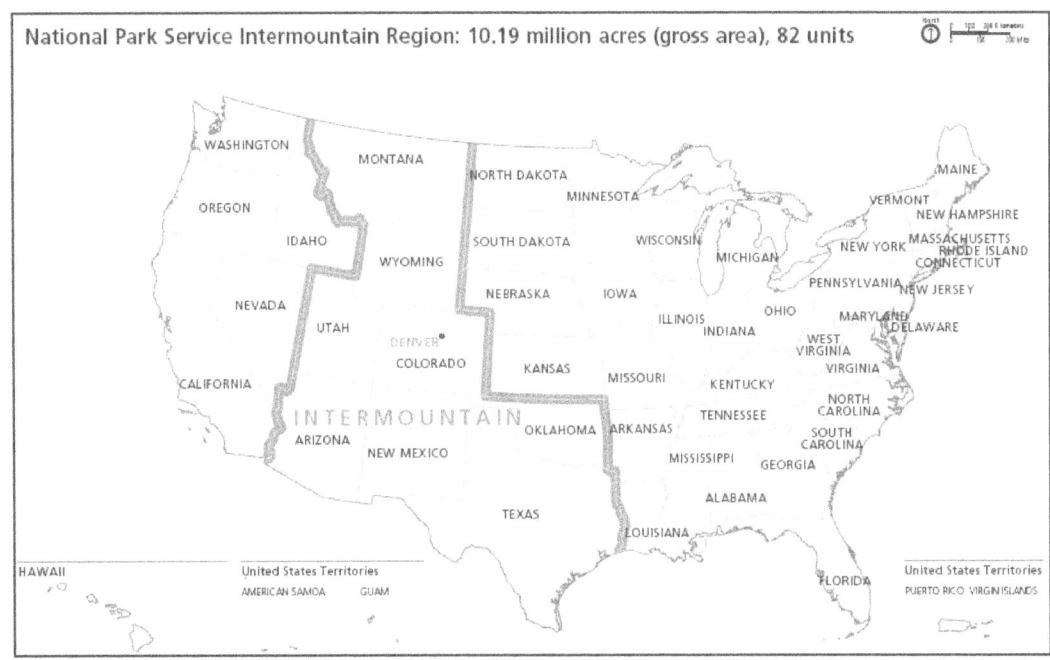

National Park Service Intermountain Region: 10.19 million acres (gross area), 82 units

Intermountain Region (IMR)

The Intermountain Region's varied environments—from barrier islands to deserts, prairies to alpine peaks—give rise to an equally diverse collection of NPS sites. The Intermountain Region identified four major focus areas to be addressed by the regional natural resource program: climate change, invasive species, renewable energy development, and border impacts. These focus areas represent major challenges to almost all parks in the region. The following accomplishments include projects that address these areas and many others.

Park Accomplishments

Arches National Park (UT): A monitoring program to record tamarisk leaf beetle (*Diorhabda* spp.) impacts, spread, and ecological parameters was implemented in conjunction with Utah's Grand County Weed Department. Preliminary monitoring results indicate that the beetle has spread through both Arches and Canyonlands National Park. Beetle impacts are causing mortality on tamarisk—an invasive, exotic species—already stressed by drought. Monitoring will continue next year. (NRPP–SP)

Bent's Old Fort National Historic Site (CO), Chickasaw National Recreation Area (OK), Lyndon B. Johnson National Historical Park (TX), Sand Creek Massacre National Historic Site (CO), Washita Battlefield National Historic Site (OK): Restoration efforts focused on removing exotic species and restoring native prairie species at these parks. Design and planning workshops and site preparation were completed prior to planting. Approximately 90 acres were restored, with an additional 67 acres planned. (NRPP–DLR)

Casa Grande Ruins National Monument (AZ): Terrestrial vegetation and soils monitoring at the monument indicated a surprising degree of site stability despite low vegetative cover and diversity. Actual and potential soil erosion was low despite the high percentages of bare surface soil due to the abundance of biological soil crusts—particularly the occurrence of light cyanobacteria. These inconspicuous organisms bind soil particles together, limiting raindrop impacts and resisting overflow of water and soil. Results illustrate how a low-key, nearly invisible organism can play a central role in protecting the finite and important archaeological treasures of a cultural resource park. (I&M)

Curecanti National Recreation Area (CO): A 10-year effort to study habitat selection of Gunnison sage-grouse (*Centrocercus minimus*), a recently listed federal candidate species, concluded in FY 2010. The goal of the study was to develop a habitat utilization model that promotes sustainable management of the Gunnison Basin sagebrush steppe ecosystem in a manner that enhances the sage-grouse population. Challenge funding was integral to supporting the sage-grouse study through the mid-2000s. In cooperation with the USGS, scientists are analyzing data and preparing manuscripts for peer-reviewed publication.

Dinosaur National Monument (CO): Using the established *Dinosaur National Monument Invasive Plant Management Plan and Environmental Assessment*, the park continued invasive plant treatment. Eighty infested acres were treated by mechanical or chemical means, and approximately 200 at-risk acres were monitored and treated with maintenance measures. Of note is the complete eradication of Russian olive (*Elaeagnus angustifolia L.*) from the monument in October 2010. (EPMT)

Gila Cliff Dwellings National Monument (NM), Chiricahua National Monument (AZ): In 2009 and 2010 Sonoran Desert Network bird monitoring added 13 new species to 11 park species lists. Gila Cliff Dwellings had the most new finds, with confirmed detections of white-winged dove, rufous-crowned sparrow, summer tanager, song sparrow, and greater pewee. One of the most notable observations was an eared quetzal (*Euptilotis neoxenus*, formerly trogon) at Chiricahua. This neotropical vagrant is native to the sky islands in central Mexico and has been observed in the United States only a handful of times. (I&M)

Glacier National Park (MT): Braided, denuded 'social' trails created a maze of linear impacts adjacent to stream banks throughout the backcountry wilderness area. Larger expanses of bare ground with compacted and eroding soils were especially significant along the route to Running Eagle Falls Overlook. A three-year project successfully restored one acre of high visitor-use impact. Work included soil stabilization; trail delineation; viewing platform construction; signs; plant materials collection, production, and installation, monitoring; and weed control. Students and volunteers assisted throughout the project. (NRPP-DLR)

Great Sand Dunes National Park and Preserve (CO): The Rocky Mountain Network completed a multi-jurisdictional vegetation classification and mapping project that covered 167,148 total hectares, including the park and preserve, adjacent Baca National Wildlife Refuge, Rio Grande National Forest, BLM-managed Blanca Wetlands, and The Nature Conservancy's Medano-Zapata Ranch. The park used the vegetation map and associated products to address bison management, invasive species, and fire management issues. (I&M)

Lake Mead National Recreation Area (AZ, NV): A multifaceted, cooperative project between the National Park Service and University of Nevada–Las Vegas Public Lands Institute, Department of Environmental and Occupational Health, and Harry Reid Center

A new vegetation map and associated products assist with fire management efforts at Great Sand Dunes National Park and Preserve, Colorado. NPS photo.

View of the Pecos National Historical Park, New Mexico, landscape including Pecos Pueblo, the Spanish Mission church, and historic pastures. NPS photo by Jill Cowley.

for Environmental Studies addressed lake issues in relation to the Water 2025 Initiative. Products included a long-term quagga mussel monitoring plan and a framework for dealing with water issues within the recreation area entitled *Long-Term Limnological and Aquatic Resource Monitoring and Research Plan for Lakes Mead and Mohave*. (CESU)

Padre Island National Seashore (TX): Park staff continued their efforts to protect the endangered Kemp's ridley sea turtle (*Lepidochelys kempii*). Seventy-four nests were found in FY 2010, the third highest number since record keeping began in 1980. Recent records seem to indicate that nesting by this species at Padre Island is becoming reestablished. Outreach efforts included 23 public hatching events with more than 5,000 visitors in attendance, 110 media interviews (double the FY 2009 number), biweekly newspaper columns, and a new social media site.

Pecos National Historical Park (NM): To identify significant historic changes to the park's environment from the contact period to the present, park staff initiated an environmental history project. Researchers from Colorado State University completed the report, entitled *Crossroads of Change: An Environmental History of Pecos NHP*, in FY 2010. Results show that the landscape changed over time due to natural factors (drought, fire, and erosion) and the influence of human settlements. (CESU)

Walnut Canyon and Wupatki National Monuments (AZ): Researchers from Northern Arizona University performed a mammal inventory, locating 48 native mammal species at each site. Significant finds include 16 species new to Walnut Canyon, including Allen's big-eared bat (*Idionycteris phyllotis*), big free-tailed bat (*Nyctinomops macrotis*), and white-backed hog-nosed skunk (*Conepatus leuconotus*), and seven new to Wupatki, including big free-tailed bat, spotted bat (*Nyctinomops macrotis*), and kit fox (*Nyctinomops macrotis*). Bighorn sheep and coati, once present historically at Walnut Canyon, no longer occur there. (CESU, I&M)

Yellowstone National Park (ID, MT, WY): A workshop in November 2009 brought together scientists and managers to identify high-priority science needs, with an emphasis on climate change, invasive species, and land use changes, in the Greater Yellowstone Area over the next 10–20 years. This effort supports the development of science agendas, which are vision documents that identify critical information gaps, steer the research community toward important science needs, and guide agencies' future funding and permitting decisions. The workshop report is available at http://greateryellowstonescience.org/gyascienceworkshop.

Noise propagation modeling, which shows how sound travels in an area, is an essential tool for understanding the acoustical conse-

Visitor enjoying Zion National Park, Utah. NPS photo.

Zion National Park's geologic hazards report.

quences of management alternatives. In FY 2010 the Natural Sounds Program conducted noise modeling to support the forthcoming winter use management plan for Yellowstone. Staff developed an interactive mapping tool for transportation noise that evaluates traffic scenarios in about a minute (about 10,000 times faster than the modeling methods used just two years ago). Results estimate that on a day when all routes are used, the sound of over-snow vehicles is audible in about 23 percent of the park. (NSP)

Zion National Park (UT): Park managers have been proactively measuring, characterizing, and studying the acoustic environment at Zion for many years in response to high levels of aviation activity over the park and the proposed replacement and expansion of a nearby airport. In FY 2010 the regional director signed the park's *Soundscape Management Plan,* the first plan prepared under NPS Director's Order #47, which requires superintendents to address the preservation of natural soundscapes and the elimination, mitigation, or minimization of inappropriate noise sources through NPS planning processes. (NSP)

With park input, the Utah Geological Survey used data assembled by the Geologic Resources Program to prepare a report entitled *Geologic Hazards of the Zion National Park Geologic-Hazard Study Area, Washington and Kane Counties, Utah* (Special Study 133). The report contains analyses of hazards from flooding, rock fall, landslides, fault ruptures, and soils. (GR)

Regional Projects

Wolverine Restoration Plan: Wolverines are a species of great conservation need, dependent on landscape-level collaboration among wildlife and land-management agencies across 10 western states. The National Park Service is part of a multi-agency, multi-NGO partnership to assess the feasibility of wolverine restoration in the southern Rockies. Staff worked with the Wildlife Conservation Society and Colorado Division of Wildlife to facilitate an inter-agency workshop that outlined specific methods for wolverine restoration in the Southern Rockies. The Wildlife Health Program led these efforts and produced a report that is being used as the basis for restoration planning efforts. (BRM)

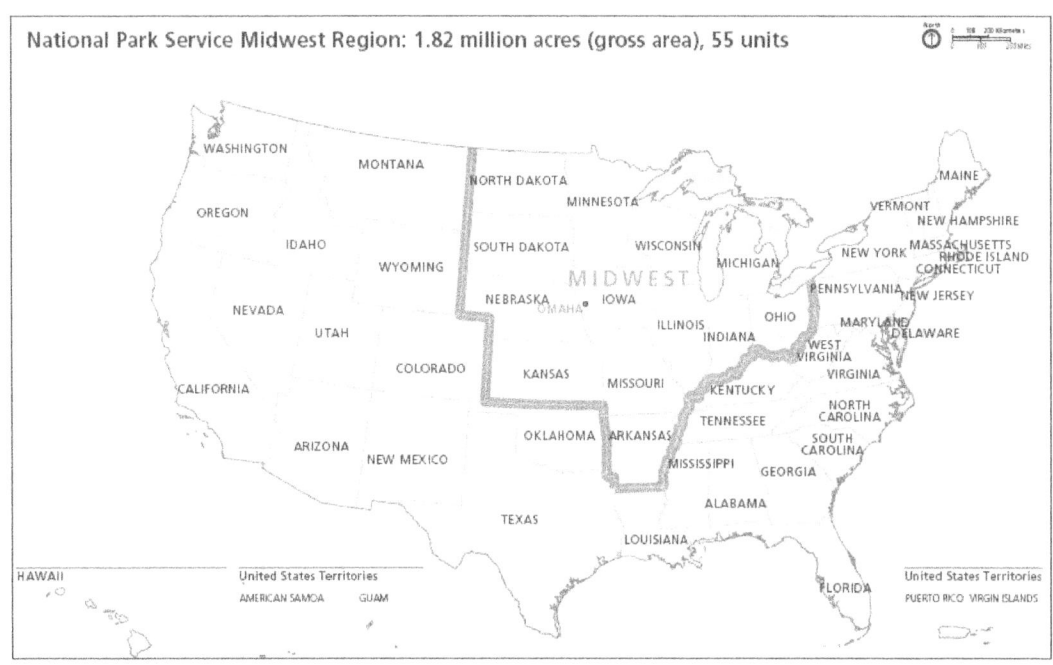

National Park Service Midwest Region: 1.82 million acres (gross area), 55 units

Midwest Region (MWR)

The parks in the Midwest Region encompass lands and waters in the Great Lakes, Great Plains, and Heartland regions of our nation. This region contains a rich heritage of lake and river ecosystems, forested plant communities, prairie landscapes, wetlands, and fish and wildlife habitats. Scientific and resource management staff in the region work to effectively manage these natural resources by integrating multiple disciplines with ecological sustainability, legal and policy requirements, and park community outreach efforts. In FY 2010 parks in the Midwest Region addressed such issues as ungulate management, invasive species, forest health, and wildlife health and disease.

Park Accomplishments

Apostle Islands National Lakeshore (WI): The insular wetlands of the Apostle Islands are ecologically unique, important for plants and animals at the edge of their range, and sensitive to potential climate change. Because of these factors, a wetland plant community inventory and assessment was performed in 1996–2001. A new project sought to determine changes in vegetation in both coastal wetlands and interior marshes and bogs in light of potential climate-related impacts and invasion by aggressive plant species. Data are being analyzed. (NRPP–RB)

Badlands National Park (SD): The swift fox (*Vulpes velox*) is a key species of the shortgrass and mixed grass prairies of the Great Plains of North America. Populations declined dramatically by the late 1800s. From 2003 to 2006, Badlands staff released 114 swift foxes to reestablish the species. A recent study assessed the long-term viability of the restored foxes, finding that the population in the park appears to be thriving, increasing from a summer population of 23 individuals in 2004 to more than 280 individuals in 2009. (NRPP–NRM)

Grand Portage National Monument (MN): A partnership between the National Park Service, Grand Portage Band of Lake Superior Chippewa, and other federal agencies identified and mitigated erosion along Grand Portage Creek using a novel approach. Successful design and installation of a biorevetment (a plant-based, living embankment) moderated stream erosion, decreased sediment deposition and enhanced water quality in Lake Superior and Grand Portage Creek, improved coaster brook trout (*Salvelinus fontinalis*) habitat, and protected cultural resources. This project represents a major advancement in stream management in the Midwest as techniques previously applied only to western waters were successfully adapted to both midwestern species and climate. (WR)

Homestead National Monument of America (NE): Resource management staff continue to monitor the white-tailed deer population. Volunteers donated more than 500 hours, taking part in monthly surveys. As part of the "Give a Day, Get a Day" program by a major amuse-

A riverbank in Grand Portage National Monument, Minnesota, before (top) and after (bottom) stabilization by biorevetment. NPS photos by Brandon Seitz.

ment park, participants came from more than 120 miles away to volunteer and in return receive free entry to the amusement park. Many volunteers had never been to the monument before, so staff used the opportunity to demonstrate the value of the monument and showcase its natural resources.

Homestead is home to the mesic bur oak forest, a rare woodland community. This critically impaired community has fewer than 20 occurrences throughout its range. A restoration project focused on the removal of exotic vegetation by temporary staff and Iowa Conservation Crew members. The woodland is now nearly free of nonnative plant species, permitting visitors to better experience the conditions the first homesteaders encountered when they arrived in eastern Nebraska. (NRPP–SP)

Hopewell Culture National Historical Park (OH): The number of acres treated for invasive plants increased fourfold in FY 2010, from 16.18 to 65.3 acres. Emphasis was placed on garlic mustard, Canada thistle, and invasive woody plants. Treatment methods included a wide range of integrated pest management practices such as hand pulling, mowing, bush-hogging, and herbicide treatments.

Indiana Dunes National Lakeshore (IN): Cowles Bog Wetland Complex, the western 205 acres of Great Marsh (Lake Michigan's largest interdunal wetland), represents the only remaining coniferous swamp associated with southern Lake Michigan, the only native population of white cedar in Indiana, and the only raised fen in Indiana without adjacent higher topographical features. Adjacent industrial development stressed the area, resulting in an 86.7 percent decline of its graminoid/forb resources between 1970 and 1982, which were replaced by non-native wetland plant species. A major restoration effort, estimated to require 10–15 years for full restoration, is now underway, including removing exotic species and planting native species. (NRPP–NRM)

Geologic Resources Program coastal staff helped park managers begin developing a shoreline management plan for Indiana Dunes National Lakeshore, the first of its kind in the National Park Service. An internal scoping meeting at the park in September 2010 brought together NPS and other federal and state partners to begin the project. The plan will address biological and physical impacts and restoration needs in the park, improving resources, visitor enjoyment, and community support. (GR)

Niobrara National Scenic River (NE): A Natural Resource Condition Assessment provided a concise synthesis and "scorecard" of the most current information about the natural resources in and around the scenic river. The assessment will help managers protect this area, often referred to as a "biological crossroads" with plant and animal species representative of northern boreal forest, eastern deciduous forest, Rocky Mountain coniferous forest, tallgrass prairie, Sandhills prairie, and mixed-grass prairie ecosystems. (CESU)

Pictured Rocks National Lakeshore (MI): To protect the federally threatened Pitcher's thistle (*Cirsium pitcheri*) and to aid in restoration of the only perched dune system on Lake Superior, more than 18 acres of spotted knapweed, red clover, white sweet clover, and other exotic plants were chemically treated within the Grand Sable Dunes Natural Research Area. Spotted knapweed (*Centaurea stoebe*) is an invasive exotic that competes with and ultimately replaces native dune vegetation, including Pitcher's thistle. (EPMT)

Pipestone National Monument (MN): A recent project inventoried and defined conditions for 1.27 acres of the monument's riparian areas, restored one acre of disturbed land, and eliminated 1.7 acres of exotic plants. Results indicate that the Pipestone Creek riparian corridor is in mostly good condition, contribute to an improved knowledge of the pattern of occurrence of the vegetation—including exotic species—along the creek, and confirm that the riparian corridor contributes to wildlife habitat. Based on project results, restoration efforts can be more targeted and efficient, saving time and money, while accelerating an eventual return to native riparian vegetative conditions. (NRPP–SP)

Saint Croix National Scenic Riverway (MN, WI), Mississippi National River and Recreation Area (MN): A partnership between the St. Croix Watershed Research Station of the Science Museum of Minnesota and the

Indiana Dunes National Lakeshore's staff constructing a water control structure (spillway) with funding provided through the Great Lakes Restoration Initiative to restore hydrology to historic wetland of the Great Marsh. NPS photo.

National Park Service, the Science Training and Research Skills program engages students in scientific research in both field and laboratory settings. In FY 2010 the program featured multiple classroom visits and three-day short programs for high school students and summer internships for undergraduates, who conducted independent research projects with the guidance of NPS research mentors. (CESU)

Theodore Roosevelt National Park (ND): The *Elk Management Plan/Environmental Impact Statement* was completed in FY 2010 to assist in the management of overabundant elk (*Cervus canadensis*) in the park. Small teams of volunteers, each led by an NPS employee, will be used to reduce elk populations to a sustainable level. Volunteers were selected by a lottery; for 240 positions, the park received applications from 5,300 individuals in 46 states. Park staff finalized other implementation details, including reduction team logistics and protocols and elk-meat issues like recovery (packing), storage, and donation. Elk reduction efforts began in October 2010.

Regional Projects
Great Lakes Restoration Initiative: The Great Lakes Restoration Initiative was established in 2010 to provide focused, coordinated funding to address the ecological health of the Great Lakes. Administered by the EPA, this inter-agency effort involves direct work by 11 federal agencies and grants to nonfederal partners. The NPS portion of the funding supported 13 projects in 11 NPS units in FY 2010; topics included contaminants, invasive species, nearshore health, and habitat and wildlife. The initiative emphasizes inter-agency collaboration and supplements base-funded activities to help accomplish work that parks would otherwise be unable to complete. The initiative has resulted in greatly expanded partnerships and multi-agency efforts to perform major restoration projects in and near the Great Lakes parks. (MWR, WRD, CESU)

Heartland Exotic Plant Network: As a major issue across the region, invasive plant species present a problem too great for any park to tackle alone. The Midwest Region established the Heartland Exotic Plant Network, an innovative dispersed team that serves multiple parks through shared park base funding.

Western Great Lakes Research Conference: More than 100 resource professionals from 24 agencies, universities, and organizations attended the eighth annual conference. A panel session on federal agency response to climate change informed conference participants and fellow agency representatives on actions each agency is taking in regards to climate change with a goal of identifying ways the Great Lakes community can collaborate on research, monitoring, management actions, and public education and outreach activities related to climate change. (CESU, I&M, RLC)

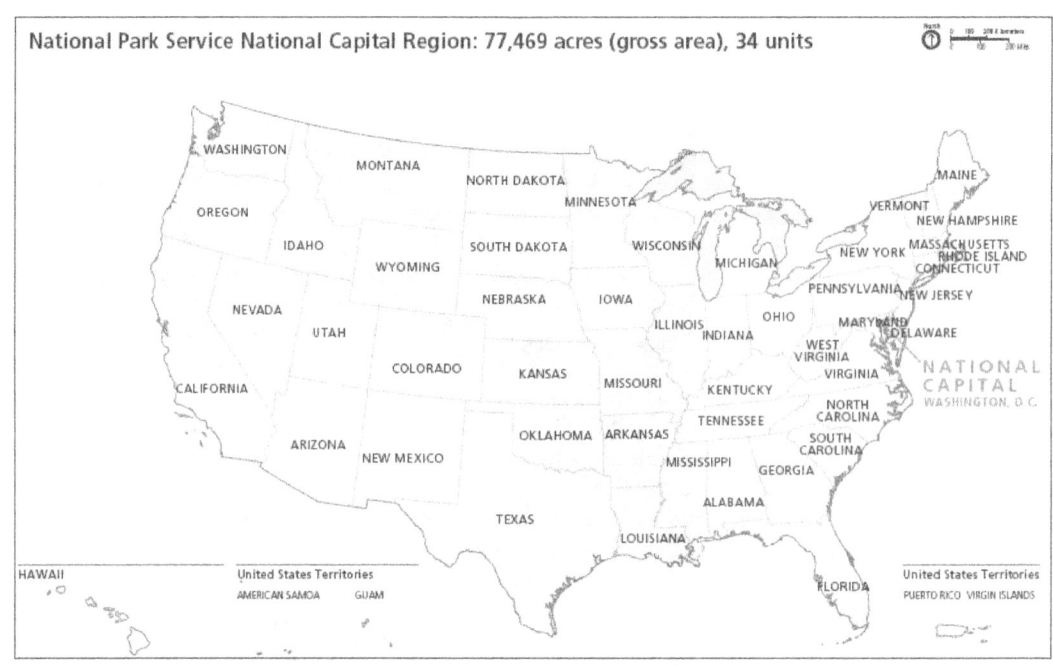

National Park Service National Capital Region: 77,469 acres (gross area), 34 units

National Capital Region (NCR)

The National Capital Region contains more than 700 individual sites, ranging from community parks that serve as neighborhood gathering places to national monuments that attract visitors from around the world. Serving more than 40 million visitors annually, the National Capital Region encompasses parkland and open space with thousands of historic structures and archeological sites; hundreds of miles of trails, historic canals, and scenic parkways; and large expanses of forests, grasslands, and riparian habitats. The top issues of specific concern to parks in the region are invasive nonnative plant management, overabundant white-tailed deer, and aquatic ecology and water resources.

Park Accomplishments

Antietam National Battlefield (MD): Staff continued the 15-year effort to improve and restore riparian buffers along all park waterways in support of park management goals and Chesapeake Bay improvement efforts. These areas serve as wildlife corridors and provide stream shade, and visitors enjoy walking the trails. In FY 2010 more than 300 volunteers planted native hardwood seedlings along a 50 foot by 3,000 foot riparian buffer along Antietam Creek. More than 2,000 trees were planted, and tree shelters were installed to protect them from browsing deer. (NRPP–SP)

Catoctin Mountain Park (MD): In 2010 Catoctin became the first park in the region to manage white-tailed deer populations based on its *White-tailed Deer Management Plan/Environmental Impact Statement* completed in 2009. The first season of white-tailed deer reduction was successfully and safely completed. Trained federal employees from USDA Wildlife Services used firearms to reduce the deer herd by 233 individuals. Following a protocol developed with the assistance of the Office of the Solicitor and Office of Public Health, approximately 4,200 pounds of meat were donated to the Maryland and Thurmont food banks.

Chesapeake and Ohio Canal National Historical Park (DC, MD, WV): The park's Indigo Tunnel is one of the state's largest hibernacula for wintering bats: the abandoned tunnel is home to eight species. Working with the Maryland Department of Natural Resources, the park is monitoring the site for signs of white nose syndrome, a deadly disease that has devastated bat populations. The tunnel is closed to public use to prevent the potential spread of white nose syndrome, and bat gates will be installed in spring 2011.

Chesapeake and Ohio Canal National Historical Park (DC, MD, WV), George Washington Memorial Parkway (DC, MD, WV), Harpers Ferry National Historical Park

(WV): The National Capital Region Network documented several species of rare plants including a colony of leatherwood (*Dirca palustris*), a regionally rare shrub and new park record on an unnamed island in Harpers Ferry; rustling wild petunia (*Ruellia strepens*), a state endangered species, in Chesapeake and Ohio Canal; and the woody vine climbing dogbane (*Trachelospermum difforme*) and an additional colony of leatherwood on Chesapeake and Ohio Canal's Sherwin Island. They also documented several plants new to the parkway, including alternate leaf dogwood (*Cornus alternifolia*), *Eupatorium sessilifolium*, *Hieracium paniculatum*, pitch pine (*Pinus rigida*), and blackjack oak (*Quercus marilandica*). (I&M)

George Washington Memorial Parkway (VA): A three-year survey in Great Falls and Turkey Run parks examined selected groups of insects that represent important bioindicators of the health of terrestrial and aquatic habitats. The study yielded interesting results, including several species likely new to science: a caddisfly (*Neophylax* sp. Nov.); a snail-killing fly (*Dictya orthi*); four shore-flies (*Hydrochasma aquia, Hydrochasma avanae, Hydrochasma garvinorum, Hydrellia toma*); a micromoth; and two species of *Aethes*. Researchers prepared an annotated species list with special focus on species that may serve conservation management. (NRPP–RB, NRPP–SP)

Smithsonian National Museum of Natural History entomologists, NPS staff, and volunteers performed a 2010 survey of beetles in Great Falls and Turkey Run parks and Dyke Marsh Wildlife Preserve. Results from this survey, in addition to thousands of beetle specimens from previous insect surveys over the past 12 years, yielded 159 beetle species representing 61 families, including seven new state records. (NRPP–RB)

Manassas National Battlefield Park (VA): A shared natural resource summer intern conducted field work at Manassas and the Virginia Department of Forestry–Conway Robinson State Forest in support of Virginia's LEAF (Link to Education about Forestry) program. This collaborative partnership developed natural resource learning opportunities at heritage tourism locations.

Monocacy National Battlefield (MD): As one of the NPS pilot sites, the battlefield completed its Resource Stewardship Strategy. The strategy is designed to guide research and resource management actions for the next 15–20 years.

Prince William Forest Park (VA): The park protects the largest expanse of Piedmont forest in the National Park System and other critical natural resources in the National Capital Region. Restoration of a 2.3-acre disturbed site, including approximately 100 meters of stream channel, helps the park return to a functioning ecosystem. A FY 2010 project worked toward this goal by removing two monitoring wells and two dams, backfill-

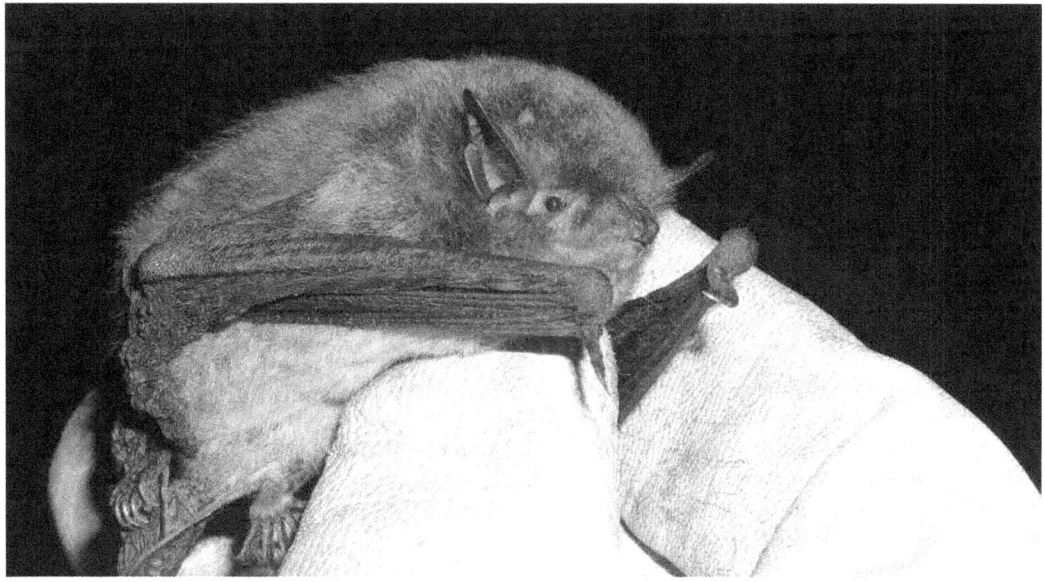

Federally endangered Indiana bat (*Myotis sodalis*) found in a mist net in front of Indigo Tunnel in Chesapeake and Ohio Canal National Historical Park. Photo by Ed Gates.

Visitors tour the native garden at Wolf Trap Farm National Park for the Performing Arts, Virginia, with park staff during a "Green Spot" event designed to educate the public about environmental issues. NPS photo.

ing two associated ponds, installing erosion control structures, removing and relocating surface and subsurface non-toxic debris, removing non-historic road beds, regrading the surrounding terrain to reestablish natural drainages, replacing topsoil, and planting native vegetation. (NRPP–DLR)

Rock Creek Park (DC): The combined efforts of park personnel, volunteers, and contractors resulted in the treatment of 559 acres of invasive plants in the park. Twenty-eight Weed Warrior volunteers and seven other volunteer groups removed invasive plants, devoting approximately 1,400 hours throughout the year. In addition, park staff and the District of Columbia Cooperative Extension in cooperation with the Casey Tree Foundation presented an invasive plant management training course to approximately 25 citizen foresters.

Wolf Trap National Park for the Performing Arts (VA): Park staff partnered with several organizations to develop a residential-scale demonstration garden using solely native plants and employing sustainable management practices. The garden educates visitors on the benefits of using native plants and demonstrates that invasive exotic species are not necessary for an attractive landscape. The garden is located at the entrance to a major attraction that receives more than 400,000 patrons each summer.

Regional Projects

Forest Bird Monitoring: National Capital Region Network observers surveyed forest birds at 385 plots across the region, conducting point counts twice throughout the season. A total of 122 species were observed across the network, including species of high conservation priority such as cerulean warblers (*Dendroica cerulean*), which are under consideration for listing as federally threatened. They also detected several Partners in Flight watch-list species. The total number of bird species recorded in network parks since monitoring began now stands at 147, including species of high conservation priority. (I&M)

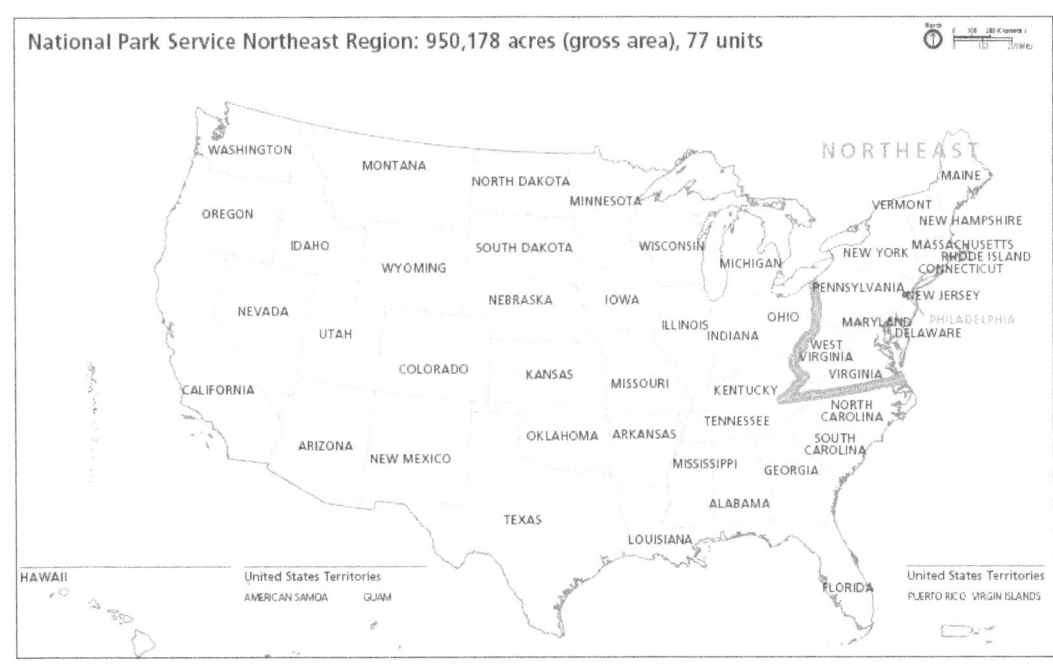

Northeast Region (NER)

The parks of the Northeast Region preserve not only the story of our nation's beginnings but also outstanding natural resources from salt marshes and seashores to rolling hills and granite mountain peaks. In FY 2010 Northeast Region parks dealt with issues common throughout the National Park Service, in particular ocean stewardship, energy development, invasive plants and insects, and climate change.

Park Accomplishments

Acadia National Park (ME): Decades of research have shown that elevated levels of mercury from atmospheric deposition exist across the park landscape. To foster awareness of the issue, park staff, science communication interns from the Schoodic Education and Research Center Institute (an NPS Research Learning Center), and the Air Resources Program worked together to create a suite of outreach products including a video podcast, fact sheet, Web pages, air quality displays, diagrams, and talking points. These communication products help translate complex, technical science about mercury patterns and effects for public audiences. (AQ, RLC)

Managers and scientists are partnering to analyze the topography of salt marshes and upland areas immediately adjacent to those marshes to determine adaptation potential for salt marshes to migrate inland as sea level rises. Twenty salt marshes were surveyed in 2010; researchers established elevation marks and reference points for further study. Results of the study will inform managers about areas needing additional protection from development and locations where man-made barriers may impede migration of the salt marshes. (CCRP)

Allegheny Portage Railroad National Historic Site (PA): The park partnered with the USFS to begin control of hemlock woolly adelgid (*Adelges tsugae*), a non-native, invasive insect pest that has caused widespread mortality and decline of eastern and Carolina hemlocks in the eastern United States. The work was conducted in hemlock-hardwood stands determined by park management to be high or medium-high priorities for control. A USFS biological evaluation assessed the condition of the stands and suggested a control strategy, which guided control actions. Follow-up treatments are planned for FY 2011.

Appalachian National Scenic Trail (ME to GA): The Appalachian Trail MEGA-Transect is a collaborative effort to gather and analyze data on air quality, water quality, wildlife habitat, forest health, land use, and nine other vital signs of the trail's environmental health. In its fourth year, the MEGA-Transect continues to attract a variety of research projects along its 2,180-mile length. Coupled with citizen science–based rare plant monitoring and invasive plant and phenology monitoring programs, the Appalachian Trail is uniquely situated to appeal to a large group of people across a broad geographic area.

Upper Delaware Scenic and Recreation River, part of the Scenic Rivers Monitoring Program partnership between the National Park Service and Delaware River Basin Commission. NPS photo by Anya Shaunessey.

Appomattox Court House National Historical Park (VA), Booker T. Washington National Monument (VA), Fredericksburg and Spotsylvania National Military Park (VA), Richmond National Battlefield Park (VA), Valley Forge National Historical Park (PA): The Mid-Atlantic Network initiated a volunteer program to monitor the status and trends of breeding bird populations. Twenty-one volunteers conducted more than 200 point counts. (I&M)

Assateague Island National Seashore (MD, VA): A 12-year vegetation monitoring project used the seashore's vegetation classification to assess habitat for the federally threatened piping plover (*Charadrius melodus*) following restoration measures to mitigate coastal erosion. Monitoring determined that previously defined thresholds of habitat loss were exceeded. The park consequently initiated measures to balance habitat maintenance with erosion mitigation. This example of using products to inform management in balancing two potentially competing resource management needs is the longest continuous application of vegetation inventory products known to date. (BRM)

Boston Harbor Islands National Recreation Area (MA): To better understand the processes of erosion, including trends, rates, and sediment volume contributions within the recreation area, a study measured coastal bluff erosion over the last half-century. Initial results indicate the highest yield per kilometer of coast is being contributed from Peddocks Island. On the other three islands in the study (Long, Thompson, and Lovells), material yields vary through time and along the coast. Impacts from seawalls and other protective structures can be seen; it is likely that such structures negatively affect the marshes through a decrease in sediment influx from the bluffs. A final report is in process. (NRPP–NRM)

Cape Cod National Seashore (MA): A shoreline change analysis examined current and past measurements of outer Cape Cod. The data will allow for assessment of present and future threats, such as sea level change, to coastal facilities and infrastructure from shoreline erosion. (NRPP–NRM)

Monitoring efforts of the Northeast Coastal and Barrier Network indicate that the emergence and breeding of spadefoot toads (*Scaphiopus h. holbrookii*), a threatened species in Massachusetts, are associated with a high groundwater table. Previously it was thought that the emergence was in response to heavy rainfall. (I&M)

Delaware Water Gap National Recreation Area (NJ, PA), Upper Delaware Scenic and

Recreation River (NY, PA): The Scenic Rivers Monitoring Program is a long-standing partnership between the Delaware River Basin Commission and the National Park Service. This monitoring-intensive program has included as many as 36 Delaware River and tributary sites, sampled biweekly May through September for 19 water quality parameters. With Special Protection Waters standards now in place for the entire 197 miles of the non-tidal Delaware River, the commission can help guide the water-intensive Marcellus Shale natural gas development in a manner that protects existing high-quality water resources for designated uses.

Gateway National Recreation Area (NY): In FY 2010 the Gateway Research Learning Center facilitated scientific research through fellowship programs focused on the effects of urbanization on both natural and sociological environments. One of these studies assessed the relationships residents from the surrounding urban areas develop with Jamaica Bay, the influence of environmental access on these relationships, and the consequences these relationships have on environmental behaviors and stewardship activities. This study will contribute valuable information to the general management plan currently underway at Gateway. (RLC)

Great Smoky Mountains National Park (NC, TN): The Appalachian Highlands Science Learning Center, in partnership with the National Park Foundation, Discover Life in America, and the National Park Service, hosted an electronic field trip on biodiversity research that was seen by 3.5 million students and teachers across North America. (RLC, CESU)

Hopewell Furnace National Historic Site (PA): The Mid-Atlantic EPMT led a pilot volunteer event at Hopewell Furnace in August 2010. It was the first volunteer event conducted at Hopewell for the purpose of invasive plant management. Eighty-eight volunteers contributed 374 hours. Media coverage of the event generated several requests for information and future collaboration. As a result, Hopewell staff hope to work with a local high school in the future. (EPMT)

New River Gorge National River (WV): In preparation for a cliff management and monitoring plan, the National Park Service is inventorying and assessing cliff resources and visitor use along the gorge wall. This area, composed of Nuttall Sandstone, is one of the premiere climbing areas in the eastern United States. The project includes trail counters, visitor observation, and botanical inventories. Research to date shows that lichen species have dominated. Data collection continues. (NRPP–NRM)

Salem Maritime National Historic Site, Saugus Iron Works National Historic Site (MA): Through a partnership with the Essex National Heritage Commission, North Shore Workforce Investment Board, and North Shore Youth Career Center, 23 local youth from minority and economically disadvantaged families worked with the National Park

F1RSTJOBS youth staff planting native sedges into the Saugus River marsh under the direction of park staff. NPS photo.

Goats grazing at Vanderbilt Mansion National Historic Site, New York, and grazed vegetation (left) compared to ungrazed areas (right). NPS photos.

Service as part of the F1RSTJOBS program. The goals of F1RSTJOBS at the parks are to develop work skills, an ethic of conservation and resource stewardship, and opportunities for youth to become future NPS employees. In FY 2010 F1RSTJOBS youth worked alongside NPS staff, including F1RSTJOBS graduates from FY 2009, on numerous natural and cultural resource projects, including native wetland planting along the Saugus River.

Vanderbilt Mansion National Historic Site (NY): The site's primary historic structures sit at the top of a steep bluff, which is difficult and dangerous to maintain using mechanized mowing equipment. A pilot program evaluated the use of goats to maintain landscapes with steep slopes. The goats were effective at grazing most plants, although staff manually removed trees to fully restore vistas. Staff plan to continue the use of livestock where feasible.

Regional Projects

Citizen Science: Citizen scientists continue to play a major role in Northeast Temperate Network monitoring activities. Sixteen skilled birders detected more than 90 species while volunteering more than 200 hours at 11 different parks; 11 volunteer birders contributed more than 150 hours at **Boston Harbor Islands National Recreation Area (MA)**; and 84 volunteers spent hundreds of hours surveying for mountain birds across the Northeast, usually on or near the **Appalachian National Scenic Trail**. Other volunteers focused on piloting the rare species protocol and phenology monitoring, participating in invasive species early detection, and conducting salt marsh vegetation and rocky intertidal monitoring. (I&M)

Early Detection of Invasive Species: The Eastern Rivers and Mountains Network and Northeast Temperate Network implemented the invasive species early detection protocol in five Northeast Region parks. The networks provided watch lists and species cards and led a training session for staff at three parks. The Northeast Temperate Network forest crew found 11 new locations of target invasive species in **Acadia National Park (ME)**, including purple loosestrife, glossy buckthorn, bush honeysuckle, Japanese barberry, and giant hogweed. (I&M)

Marcellus Shale Gas Development: The Geologic Resources Program helped parks address many issues surrounding development of the vast gas resources of the Marcellus Shale, which extends from southern New York to Virginia and eastern Ohio. Development of Marcellus Shale resources eventually may adversely affect 35 units of the National Park System and a number of special status areas. In FY 2010 the report *Development of the Natural Gas Resources in the Marcellus Shale* was updated to inform interested parties about the technological, environmental, and policy aspects of Marcellus Shale exploration and development. (GR)

Marine Habitat Mapping: Marine habitat mapping represents a critical inventory need for coastal parks and is required for the effective protection, restoration, and research of marine resources within coastal park boundaries. The North Atlantic Coast CESU held a workshop to educate park managers on state-of-the-art marine habitat mapping techniques, introduce managers to experts in this discipline, and prepare managers to develop funding proposals. The workshop was a collaborative effort with other federal land management agencies, including the USFWS and NOAA. (CESU)

Potential National Natural Landmarks: A research team from the University of Richmond and University of Maryland Center for Environmental Science evaluated potential National Natural Landmarks in the region, focusing on sites that feature underrepresented NPS themes. They identified potential sites with excellent illustrative character within four physiographic provinces of the Northeast Region—the Appalachian Plateau, Appalachian Ranges, Piedmont, and Coastal Plain—and evaluated two potential sites.

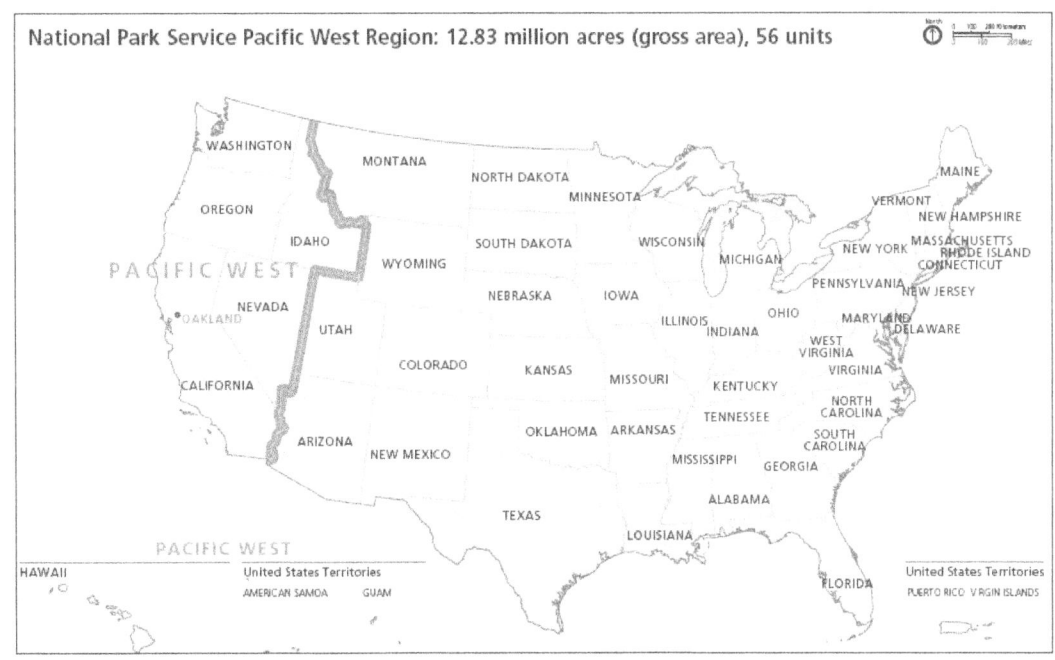

National Park Service Pacific West Region: 12.83 million acres (gross area), 56 units

Pacific West Region (PWR)

Rich in cultural and natural diversity, the Pacific West Region extends across more than 100 degrees longitude, encompassing a network of NPS units from eastern Nevada to Guam and Saipan on the other side of the International Date Line. Issues of concern to the Pacific West Region include climate change, ocean stewardship, invasive exotic species, ecosystem fragmentation, preservation of rare and endangered species, increasing demand for energy development and water use, and relevancy of parks to the public. To address these difficult issues the region builds partnerships with stakeholders and seeks funds for research, monitoring, and management programs designed to maximize natural resource protection and ecosystem resilience.

Park Accomplishments

Channel Islands National Park (CA): Work continues on the restoration of three endangered subspecies of island fox (*Urocyon littoralis*) in the park. Predation by golden eagles in spring 2010 caused annual survival to decline to 60 percent on Santa Rosa Island, reducing the population by 10–25 percent. In 2010 island foxes on the northern Channel Islands numbered above 1,500. Two of the three subspecies are close to meeting biological criteria for de-listing, all prior to the release of a recovery plan by the USFWS. This represents one of the fastest recoveries of any listed species.

City of Rocks National Reserve (ID): A nonfunctional irrigation pipe along the eastern side of the reserve represented a safety and environmental threat. The pipe was a hazard to people and horses on a reserve trail, likely compromised water quality through oxidation, and was incompatible with the California Trail Management Zone in which it was located. Staff removed and recycled the 1,500-foot pipe.

Golden Gate National Recreation Area (CA): New benthic habitat and geologic maps were developed to help staff learn more about the area's submerged resources. These maps serve as a basis for protecting marine and estuarine resources and support NPS goals for coastal resource stewardship in parks. (CESU, I&M)

Geologic Resources Program staff provided support at Golden Gate in response to storm damage. The City of San Francisco declared a state of emergency for a section of the Great Highway next to Ocean Beach and NPS land. Program staff reviewed the proposed stabilization alternatives and preliminary design drawings developed by a consulting firm and provided feedback about the potential impacts to park resources. (GR)

Great Basin National Park (NV): Park staff partnered with The Nature Conservancy to develop a conservation action plan that uses

Installing fences as part of a feral animal removal program at Kalaupapa National Historical Park, Hawaii. NPS photo.

satellite imagery to map the current and potential condition of plant communities. Predictive ecological models and cost-benefit assessments were then developed for each plant community. Climate models were incorporated to allow for scenario planning. The final product will allow the park to prepare a science-based vegetation management plan and complete climate change scenario planning.

Haleakala National Park (HI): The native Hawaiian snail Hihiwai (*Neritina granosa*) and Hihiwai eggs were documented in the park for the first time in more than 15 years. Previous surveys had failed to locate this snail in the park. Hihiwai are culturally significant animals, used as a food source extensively throughout the Hawaiian Islands. Increased collecting of Hihiwai reduced populations significantly, extirpating them from some streams entirely. This find indicates the potential for this native species to reestablish a population in Palikea Stream within the park. (I&M)

John Day Fossil Beds National Monument (OR): In partnership with the National Marine Fisheries Service, BLM, and Oregon Natural Desert Association, a project to increase threatened steelhead (*Oncorhynchus mykiss*) populations in the Bridge Creek watershed continued. One priority of the project is to restore native riparian vegetation. In spring 2010 approximately 1,400 native tree cuttings were planted along Bridge Creek and 85 trees were planted along the John Day River.

Kalaupapa National Historical Park (HI): An increasing feral goat population was rapidly degrading and deforesting historically pristine sea cliffs in the park. An aerial shooting program had conditioned the animals to retreat into forested areas. Staff employed a combination of fencing, aerial shooting, and hunting to remove the goats, as well as nonnative deer and pigs, from the cliffs. More than 350 feral ungulates were removed from the area. (NRPP–NRM)

Lassen Volcanic National Park, Sequoia and Kings Canyon National Parks, Yosemite National Park (CA): The National Park Service is working with federal and state partners to compile and assess existing databases for information on the deposition and accumulation of toxic air contaminants in sensitive resources across all federal and state lands in the Sierra Nevada–Southern Cascades region. The resultant toxic air contaminants research and monitoring strategy will inform managers and the public about the conditions and trends of toxic air contaminants and associated sensitive receptors. (AQ)

Mojave National Preserve (CA): Preserve staff continued their efforts to protect the federally threatened desert tortoise (*Gopherus agassizii*) from death on paved roads due to direct vehicle impact. A multi-year study confirmed the USFWS opinion that road kill of tortoises in the preserve is a problem and that warning signs and increased awareness have little effect. Barrier fencing may be necessary to protect the tortoises.

The Mohave tui chub (*Siphateles bicolor mohavensis*), the only fish species native to the Mojave River, was listed as endangered in 1970. Its extirpation is thought to result from hybridization and subsequent introgression with the introduced arroyo chub (*Gila orcutti*). Recently a third species, *Lavinia exilicauda*, gained access to the river and hybridized with arroyo chub. Preserve staff and the California Department of Fish and Game started a collaborative study with geneticists at Texas A&M University–Corpus Christi to reexamine the viability of hybrids in anticipation of reintroducing Mohave tui chub into the headwaters of the Mojave River. Results of this research will guide ongoing recovery efforts to establish new populations of the endangered fish. (NRPP–RB)

North Cascades National Park (WA): North Coast and Cascades Network staff collaborated with park interpreters to develop an electronic field trip. Funded through the National Park Foundation, "Climate Challenge: North Cascades National Park" reached more than 150,000 students and teachers. The field trip included web-based interactive games and lesson plans that explored climate change and its effects on people and ecosystems. The archived broadcast, games, and lessons plans are available at www.northcasdeseft.org. (I&M)

The Cascades Climate Challenge, funded through North Cascades Institute Program, inspires and equips the next generation of climate stewards with knowledge of field-based climate change science and the tools necessary to be effective leaders and communicators. North Coast and Cascades Network staff shared their expertise in monitoring with high school students from Washington and northern Oregon, who spent three weeks in the park and surrounding forest. Presentations featured locally collected data and climate change information relevant to the students' lives and exposed them to NPS careers in science. (I&M)

Olympic National Park (WA): Fishers (*Martes pennanti*), extirpated throughout Washington by the late 20th century, are candidates for listing as federally endangered. In the third year of a 10-year, multi-agency project

Mojave National Preserve and California Department of Fish and Game staff collecting pure Mohave tui chub for use in laboratory and pond experiments to evaluate the potential for hybridization between the endangered Mohave tui chub and the introduced arroyo chub.

to restore fishers to Washington, the ninetieth fisher was released into the park. Fishers have successfully dispersed throughout the Olympic Peninsula. Successful reproduction in the wild has been documented for the past two years. The second phase of the project will assess if the reintroduced population persists, grows, and is suitable to serve as a source population for reintroduction into other portions of its former range in Washington.

Preparations have begun for the removal of two hydroelectric dams on the Elwha River. The dam removals are part of the Elwha River Restoration Project, which is intended to restore the river and associated watershed and coastal ecosystems, including the historic anadromous fishery. In FY 2010 heavy equipment was used to remove vegetation and construct a pilot channel down the center of the delta at the head of Lake Mills. Restoration of fluvial landscapes and processes through this area requires effective erosion and redistribution of the delta sediments by the river. Dam removal is scheduled to begin in fall 2011. (WR)

Point Reyes National Seashore (CA): Prior to the seashore's establishment, rock was extracted from numerous quarries within its current boundaries for the construction of features such as roads and stock pond dams. To ensure public safety, end unauthorized removal of rock, establish native vegetation on disturbed lands, and diminish impacts from storm water runoff, seven quarries were reclaimed and restored between 2007 and 2010. Approximately 7.5 acres of disturbed lands were restored, more than 240 pounds of seed were sown, and nearly 65,000 container plants were planted. (NRPP–DLR)

Redwood National and State Parks (CA): The park performed restoration thinning of second-growth forests in the South Fork Lost Man Creek watershed to reduce overall stand density, accelerate development of understory vegetation, and alter species composition to favor redwoods. Without thinning, these impaired forests were likely to languish as dense thickets of undersized trees that bore little resemblance to the old growth forests that stood prior to the harvest. This program is unique in the scale of forest restoration activities, which is greater than what other parks have attempted.

Santa Monica Mountains National Recreation Area (CA): A free iPhone application was developed through a collaborative partnership between NPS staff and researchers at the University of California–Los Angeles. The application enables a user to photograph invasive plants within the park and transmit the

Lake Mills delta and Elwha River in Olympic National Park, Washington, November 2010.

Release of a Sierra green sulphur butterfly, endemic to the Sierra Nevada, as part of a survey to estimate population size at Yosemite National Park through the Californian CESU. Photo by Sean Schoville.

photo with the embedded GPS coordinates to park staff. The photos are verified and automatically added to a GIS map and database for tracking the presence and spread of invasive species. This novel, high-tech approach works particularly well in an urban setting with ample cell phone coverage and high visitation, though it is also portable to other parks. The Mediterranean Coast Network will incorporate the technology into I&M protocol development. (I&M)

Sequoia and Kings Canyon National Parks (CA): The parks are working with researchers to understand the dynamics of carbon cycling in forest ecosystems. The dynamic approach involves coring trees in areas burned under four levels of fire severity (including unburned areas) and comparing the carbon accumulation rates. Results will inform fire management in this complex system. (CCRP)

Yosemite National Park (CA): Results of a three-year study of alpine butterflies provide critical information for tracking future alpine butterfly population trends and assessing the influences of environmental changes on the park's alpine butterfly community. The study also improves knowledge of the population ecology, taxonomic status, and evolutionary history of two of Yosemite's more rare alpine butterflies, Sierra Nevada parnassian (*Parnassius behrii*) and Sierra green sulphur (*Colias behrii*). (CESU)

Regional Projects

Multi-Network Pine Monitoring Protocol: The Upper Columbia Basin, Sierra Nevada, and Klamath I&M networks completed a monitoring protocol to estimate status and trends in the population dynamics of high-elevation whitebark, limber, and foxtail pine species. Whitebark pine is being decimated by the non-native white-pine blister rust and outbreaks of mountain pine beetle in many parts of the western United States. To a lesser extent, limber pine and foxtail pines, species closely related to whitebark pine, have also been impacted by these infections and are increasingly vulnerable under predictions of accelerated climate change. (I&M)

Recruiting Diverse Students: The Southern California Research Learning Center hosted several interactive exhibits aimed at recruiting promising Hispanic students into careers in the National Park Service. The center also uses experiential distance education tools (e.g., interactive video feeds) to reach underserved audiences. (RLC)

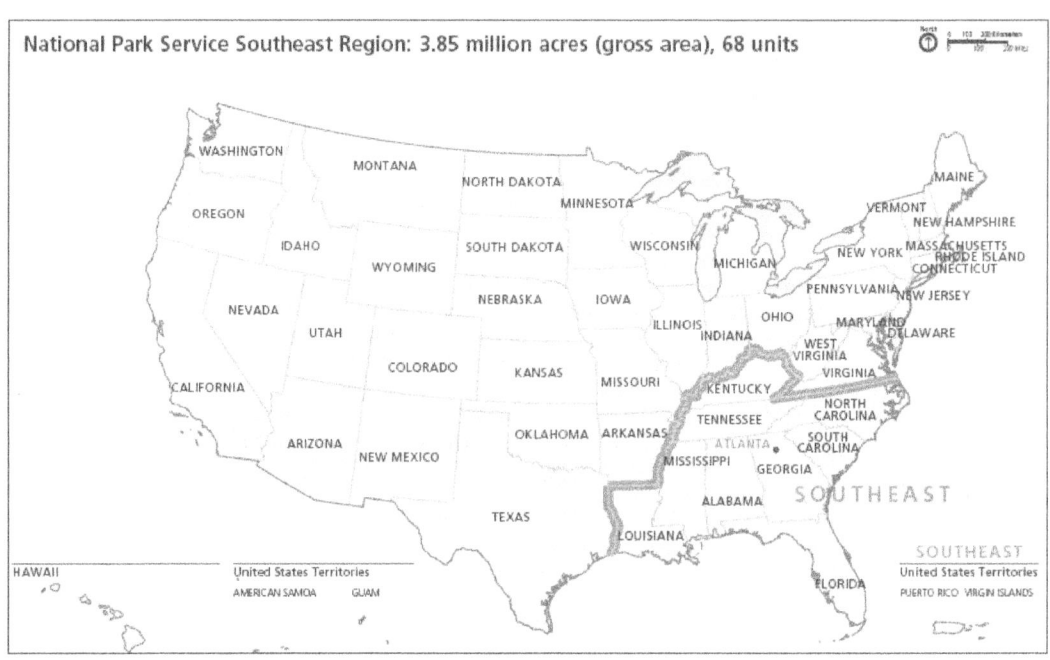

National Park Service Southeast Region: 3.85 million acres (gross area), 68 units

Southeast Region (SER)

While two-thirds of the NPS units in the Southeast Region feature history as their primary theme, the region's natural treasures include biodiversity hotspots in the Great Smoky Mountains and Everglades and five of 10 national seashores.

Park Accomplishments

Biscayne National Park (FL): The fourth annual National Park Service–National Geographic BioBlitz was held on April 30–May 1, 2010. A record number of participants, including 1,300 students and educators from elementary to university levels, 200 volunteers, and more than 170 scientists and experts, conducted inventories of the park's four major ecosystems. Teachers, students, and local residents explored and documented park resources in the field with scientists, and many new volunteers learned about service opportunities available at the park. Scientists documented a preliminary tally of 828 species, 324 of which are new listings on the park's official species list. (BRM, I&M)

Blue Ridge Parkway (NC, VA), Great Smoky Mountains National Park (NC, TN): An aquatic macroinvertebrate collected during surveys by the Appalachian Highlands Network was described as an entirely new genus known only from a single spring on the parkway in Virginia. Other significant aquatic macroinvertebrate records were published this year as a result of network surveys at Blue Ridge Parkway and USGS surveys at Great Smoky Mountains, including 41 new state records for caddisflies in North Carolina. (I&M)

Buck Island Reef National Monument (Virgin Islands): The monument conducts an annual reef fish census in partnership with NOAA. Field staff conducted more than 130 surveys, determining habitat condition and reef fish diversity and abundance both inside and adjacent to park boundaries. These data help the park determine if the marine reserve is working to improve the reef fishery.

Canaveral National Seashore (FL): The University of Florida initiated a study to assess the communities and resource uses by contemporary peoples within the seashore. Additionally university researchers and students are working with NPS staff to provide an overview of the archaeological or prehistoric research conducted in the seashore in an effort to identify and protect natural and cultural resources that have special significance for peoples and communities associated with park lands. The study involves collaboration with the Miccosukee and Seminole tribes. (CESU)

Cape Lookout National Seashore (NC): A storm hazard recovery plan was drafted for the seashore, outlining protocols for short-, medium-, and long-range management actions for resource recovery. Other coastal parks, management agencies, and local communities can adapt and use the plan and its components to enhance the recovery and preservation of natural and cultural resources. (CESU, GR)

Chattahoochee River National Recreation Area (GA): Restoration of the 25-acre Johnson Ferry wetlands was completed this year. The wetlands are significant ecologically, archaeologically, and socially. The Georgia Corporate Wetland Restoration Partnership, a Coastal America initiative, selected the wetlands for the state's first project. The final year of the project involved monitoring trends in water quality, stream condition, vegetation, fish, and macroinvertebrate communities. Channel stabilization improved two streams flowing into the Chattahoochee River by allowing aquatic species to move between the wetland and river and by recreating an intact riparian environment. (GR, NRPP–DLR)

Cumberland Island National Seashore (GA): Fifteen artesian wells in the seashore tap into the deep Floridian Aquifer. Eight of these wells are abandoned and are no longer maintained. A two-year project is underway to plug or cap five abandoned wells, mitigating the loss of more than 34 million gallons of groundwater annually and restoring the terrestrial habitat adjacent to each well. (NRPP–RB)

Dry Tortugas National Park (FL): A three-year science report was produced for the Dry Tortugas Research Natural Area and Special Protection Zones Conservation Assessment project. The report summarizes the progress of science plan activities to date. The research natural area is a no-take, no-anchoring marine reserve established to protect shallow water habitats and reef fish species. (NRPP–NRM)

Great Smoky Mountains National Park (NC, TN): Park staff and volunteers treated 57 acres of invasive exotic plants in FY 2010, including 459 of 833 sites identified as targeted areas, and mapped 345 sites using updated GIS technology. Full-time volunteers, including three Student Conservation Association interns, a retired civil engineer, and one AmeriCorps team, contributed significantly. Activities included hand-pulling, foliar spraying with selective herbicides, cut/stump herbicide treatments, and monitoring.

Brook trout (*Salvelinus fontinalis*), known to occupy nearly 440 miles of streams in the park prior to European settlement, now occupy less than 30 percent of their former range. Early logging, the introduction and encroachment of non-native rainbow trout, and more recently acid precipitation caused the majority of the loss. The park's *Fishery Management*

Scientist leading students on a plant walk at the Biscayne National Park BioBlitz. NPS photo by Thomas M. Strom.

Re-establishment of vegetation in marshlands at Jean Lafitte National Historical Park and Preserve, Louisiana, after restoration of oil and gas development canals. NPS photo.

Plan identifies restoration of their historic range as a high priority for the protection and conservation of native brook trout. Restoration of the Lynn Camp Prong watershed was underway when surveys discovered illegally stocked rainbow trout in the project area. FY 2010 efforts focused on removing all rainbow trout from the area so that restoration of brook trout can continue.

Jean Lafitte National Historical Park and Preserve (LA): Fifteen miles of abandoned oil and gas development access canals were backfilled using "floating excavators" to restore natural hydrologic function on approximately 15 acres of marshland. Use of floating excavators is a unique practice that has proven to be highly technically and cost effective at restoring these very productive wetlands. The project also removed invasive plant species from the canal berms. Reestablishment of marsh elevation created conditions that will allow natural revegetation of appropriate plant communities. (GR)

Little River Canyon National Preserve (AL): Staff worked with the state biologist to determine native species suitable for converting planted wildlife openings into grass fields and an old field at **Russell Cave National Monument (AL)** into a wildflower meadow. With the help of the Blue Ridge EPMT, staff treated the fields and readied them for planting in 2011.

Mammoth Cave National Park (KY): A draft report for vegetation communities and plant inventories informed several resource management projects, including a new study on fire history and pre-settlement vegetation. Ecologists identified 42 ecological community types; 32 are "natural" communities and, of these, six are globally rare. Four of the rare communities are related to exposures of limestone or other habitats favorable to light-demanding plants. In addition, botanists identified 79 new species not previously documented, bringing the total to 1,185 species for the park. (I&M)

Obed Wild and Scenic River (TN): A new streamflow gauge on the upper Obed River broadcasts, via satellite, river stage and discharge data and near real-time water quality data to a USGS website. This gauge allows the park to further document water quality and streamflow conditions in preparation for future water resources projects, some of which could affect the park.

Stones River National Battlefield (TN): Located in one of the fastest-growing counties in the country, the battlefield continued efforts to restore and preserve native grasslands. Sixty-eight acres were converted to and managed for native grasses over the past three years; an additional 34 acres will be converted. This work moves a significant portion of battlefield property toward a desired future condition, creates

NPS divers with a speared invasive lionfish at Lameshur Bay, St. John, in the U.S. Virgin Islands. NPS photo.

a more sustainable landscape, restores the cultural landscape to its general 1860s appearance, and improves wildlife habitat. (NRPP–SP)

Virgin Islands National Park (Virgin Islands): In 2010 the first exotic marine fish appeared in the park. The invasive lionfish (*Pterois volitans*), native to the western Pacific, Indian Ocean, and Red Sea, invaded the western Atlantic and Caribbean in the last five years. During 2010 eight lionfish were removed from park waters. This is the beginning of a major invasion by a species that will have highly detrimental effects on coral reefs and native fish populations in the park and throughout the region.

Water temperatures in the U.S. Virgin Islands never cooled from 2009 summer temperatures and began heating up during the spring and early summer of 2010. These increased ocean temperatures exceeded the historical data range and triggered a coral bleaching event. Hurricane activity reduced water temperatures somewhat; with temperatures exceeding the critical threshold, however, South Florida/Caribbean Network staff began additional coral monitoring to document the level of bleaching. (I&M)

Regional Projects
Border Issues: Park managers in South Florida deal with issues specific to land managers along the U.S. international border, including illegal border crossings, drug smuggling, resource impacts, pollution, and hazardous waste disposal resulting from smuggling activities. A project launched in FY 2010 at **Everglades National Park (FL)** will document the variety and magnitude of international border issues germane to the park as a scoping exercise, which will help inform NPS efforts to strategically address the international border issues faced by NPS units in South Florida and the Caribbean.

Cooperative Invasive Species Management: Hundreds of invasive species have been introduced into Florida. National parks have been instrumental in establishing a cooperative invasive species management area with a memorandum of understanding to guide invasive species efforts in the greater Everglades area. This cooperative effort among federal, state, tribal, and non-governmental organizations features a standardized treatment and reporting database and a rapid response plan for plants and animals. Partners implemented digital aerial sketch mapping technology, facilitating monitoring on more than 20 million acres in South Florida. The focus on coordinated efforts has led to early detection of new invasive species, including two species of tegus, a lizard native to South America. (BRM)

Linking Inventory and Monitoring with Climate Science: The Southeast Coast Network has entered into a long-term cooperative agreement with the University of Georgia to house the Southeast Coast Network/South Atlantic Landscape Conservation Cooperative (LCC) and Climate Science Support Center. The program management, data management, water quality, and climate science portions of the Southeast Coast Network and the South Atlantic Refuges I&M Program will share the office to facilitate the standardization of monitoring methods, integration of data systems, and coordination with the South Atlantic LCC and Southeastern DOI Climate Science Center. The intent is to develop a network of approximately 50 land units across the Southeast Coast and South Atlantic Refuge networks where managers can use I&M data to better inform planning decisions at the park/refuge level and the landscape scale as the agencies and their partners develop strategies to respond to climate change. (I&M)

Chapter 4: Servicewide Accomplishments

By focusing efforts on the broad issues, such as climate change, ocean stewardship, biodiversity, and energy development, that affect NPS resources, Servicewide natural resource programs reach across state and regional boundaries to provide benefits for multiple parks and regions.

Airborne Contaminants in the West: The Western Airborne Contaminants Assessment Project (WACAP), which ended in 2007, yielded multiple science and policy benefits in FY 2010. The study assessed the extent and impacts of toxic compounds in 19 western national park ecosystems. Results contributed to the EPA's 2010 decision to prohibit all uses of the pesticide endosulfan in the United States. Data were also used by the EPA and the Department of State to inform international contaminant recommendations for the 2010 Stockholm Convention on Persistent Organic Pollutants. A comprehensive article describing key WACAP results was published in the journal *Environmental Science and Technology* in January 2010, and the complete database was made available for download. (AQ)

Assistance for Ocean and Coastal Issues: The description and analysis of NPS jurisdiction, authorities, boundaries, and remedies are necessary to increase technical capacity in the Ocean and Coastal Resources Program. A contract was awarded to conduct research and develop park-specific legal memoranda regarding the location and modification of unit boundaries. Park units included in these analyses are faced with sea- and lake-level changes, dynamic geologic features and coastal processes, and other factors that necessitate analysis of unit boundaries. The resulting legal memoranda will be used by the NPS Land Resources Division to update park boundaries and by other NPS offices to help parks apply available authorities within the updated boundaries. (WR)

Benefits Sharing: The National Park Service convened a Servicewide team to develop the benefits-sharing program selected in March 2010 in a court-ordered environmental impact statement and record of decision. Under this program, the National Park Service would negotiate and enter into agreements with researchers or institutions that anticipate a commercial application of research results from previously permitted research activity in NPS units. Benefits sharing, which was authorized by the National Parks Omnibus Management Act of 1998, could return scientific benefits, non-monetary services, and monetary payments to parks when research results lead to the development of commercially valuable products. (GR)

Biodiversity Discovery: The term "Biodiversity Discovery" encompasses a variety of efforts to discover and document our natural heritage. More than 40 park units have conducted different types of Biodiversity Discovery activities, including All-Taxa Biodiversity Inventories that document all species in a geographic area, BioBlitzes that search for species within a given—often 24-hour—timeframe, and Bioquests that focus on more targeted activities such as an afternoon collecting rare plants. In FY 2010 the National Park Service and National Geographic Society were awarded DOI's Partners in Conservation Award for their commitment and support of annual large-scale BioBlitzes in parks near urban areas, including the 2010 **Biscayne National Park (FL)** BioBlitz (page 48). (BRM)

Bison Conservation: A group of bison experts from across the United States prepared a state-of-knowledge report of DOI bison genetics in support of the Bison Conservation Initiative, signed into effect in 2008 to guide DOI bison stewardship. Once a symbol of the American West, only several thousand wild and free-ranging bison remain. Most of these are under DOI stewardship. (BRM)

Climate Change Youth Initiative: The George Melendez Wright Climate Change Internship and Fellowship programs placed 13 interns and 22 fellows in parks and offices across the country. Designed to harness the energy and creativity of undergraduate and graduate students, the new programs support-

Bison at Grand Teton National Park, Wyoming. Photo by Jerry Megenity.

Climate change intern in Rocky Mountain National Park, Colorado.

ed a range of park-based research, resource management, energy efficiency, and climate change communication projects. (CCRP)

Climate Change Response Strategy: The Servicewide *Climate Change Response Strategy* was released in September 2010. The strategy emphasizes four key elements—science, adaptation, mitigation, and communication—and stresses the need for a legal and policy framework to guide planning and implementation for climate change. The goals and objectives outlined in the strategy will guide development of a detailed implementation plan in 2011. (CCRP)

Coastal Engineering Inventory Report: A reconnaissance-level report of coastal engineering projects for 10 national park units (Apostle Islands National Lakeshore [WI], Boston Harbor Islands National Recreation Area [MA], Cape Lookout National Seashore [NC], Channel Islands National Park [CA], Fire Island National Seashore [NY], Fort Pulaski National Monument [GA], Indiana Dunes National Lakeshore [IN], Jean Lafitte National Historical Park [LA], Lewis and Clark National Historical Park [OR, WA], and Timucuan Ecological and Historic Preserve [FL]) was completed in September 2010. (GR)

Communicating Soundscape Issues: A special issue of *Park Science*, a research and resource management bulletin of the National Park Service, addressed the results of research efforts to develop an evolving conceptual model of soundscapes in parks. The issue won an Apex Award of Publication Excellence for 2010. (NSP)

Geoscientists-in-the-Parks (GIP) Program: In FY 2010 59 GIP participants worked in 29 parks and two central offices covering all NPS regions. Participants directly reached park visitors through geologic outreach and education programs, improvements to park websites, and other outreach materials. The FY 2010 program leveraged federal dollars at a rate of five to one, with the National Park Service receiving more than $1.45 million in project work at a cost of about $292,000. (GR)

Learning about Pests: Two technology-enhanced learning broadcasts taught NPS participants Servicewide about invasive pests. "Firewood: A Threat to Forest Resources" provided steps employees should take to reduce the risk of transporting invasive pests in firewood. "Bed Bugs…Beds and Beyond: Learn the Facts" dispelled bedbug myths and provided practical prevention, detection, and low-risk management strategies. Educational efforts such as these help reduce unnecessary pesticide use, lessen associated risks, and foster improved resource management. (BRM)

Ocean and Coastal Workshop: In FY 2010 the Geologic Resources and Water Resources programs published the report of the 2009 NPS Ocean Workshop. Work began on clarifying ambiguous park boundaries, refining the coastal jurisdiction handbook, supporting development of sediment management guidance, clarifying water quality protection standards, and developing an NPS ocean and coastal director's order. (GR, WR)

Partners in Flight: Partners in Flight is a collection of individuals and groups who share a vision of healthy bird populations. Partners include government agencies, private businesses, academic institutions, chambers of commerce, and private citizens. International Migratory Bird Day, held on May 8, 2010, is an annual outreach and education event that brings attention to factors that contribute to the decline in world bird populations. (BRM)

Partnership Activities: The natural resources partnership program provides increased and targeted partnership and philanthropy development for natural resource initiatives. In FY 2010 these partnerships enhanced and maintained the Air Quality Web Camera Network and supported the development of an activity about the waters in national parks for the *ProjectWet Curriculum and Activity Guide* for students in grades K–12.

White-Nose Syndrome: Identified as an emerging national wildlife crisis with more than one million hibernating bats in caves and mines killed by the disease, a national committee of wildlife biologists, park cave and abandoned mine specialists, and natural resources staff developed guidance and provided recommendations for preventing the spread of this disease by human transmission within NPS units. The committee's work led to national guidance that offers park units specific goals to help limit the spread of the disease. Managers hope the guidance will help slow the spread of the disease to give scientists and researchers time to better understand the disease and develop protocols to save as many hibernating bats as possible. (BRM, GR)

Wildlife and Research: The NPS Animal Care and Use Committee enhanced the ability of the National Park Service to ensure the most humane treatment of wildlife used in research in the parks. In its inaugural year, the committee assessed 16 animal use projects in 18 NPS units representing five regions and involving numerous species of mammals, birds, and amphibians.

Appendix A: Natural Resource Challenge Funding in Parks

Table A-1. Natural resource funding of National Park Service units receiving Natural Resource Challenge increases in FY 2001 or FY 2002

NPS unit	Amount of Challenge Increase ($)	Natural resource total ($)								
		FY 2002	FY 2003	FY 2004	FY 2005	FY 2006	FY 2007	FY 2008	FY 2009	FY 2010
Acadia NP	345,000	849,827	794,395	755,087	752,395	695,273	726,254	722,433	795,278	826,276
Antietam NB	150,000	319,965	316,723	314,900	353,000	350,000	420,000	421,360	425,000	477,000
Appalachian NST	142,000	263,638	256,603	258,337	298,642	299,453	310,919	316,667	273,351	273,351
Big Cypress NPr	399,000	1,033,640	1,010,000	1,108,140	1,108,140	1,085,907	1,104,663	1,050,220	841,536	1,277,054
Buck Island Reef NM	100,000	270,000	216,450	216,000	216,000	216,000	216,000	216,000	216,000	216,000
Catoctin Mountain Park	89,000	254,400	231,900	232,200	272,414	174,867	200,594	204,976	370,829	407,931
Channel Islands NP	498,000	1,406,622	1,406,622	1,440,607	1,891,222	1,891,222	1,891,222	2,255,648	2,487,208	2,479,877
Coronado N Mem	60,000	94,993	105,231	95,236	108,000	60,000	60,000	60,000	60,000	60,000
Curecanti NRA	141,000	657,500	690,600	719,300	724,000	731,700	741,900	859,100	894,800	1,126,358
Dinosaur NM	189,000	501,800	559,375	568,874	571,152	524,200	627,280	772,738	667,000	673,000
Gates of the Arctic NP and Pr[a]	148,000	362,401	363,039	349,164	377,345	357,517	342,014	534,945	533,000	475,665
Great Basin NP	126,000	331,450	315,756	375,939	367,080	382,600	454,600	483,157	498,319	560,829
Great Sand Dunes NP and Pr	180,000	291,700	287,500	281,300	281,300	323,400	332,000	325,300	344,900	364,300
Great Smoky Mountains NP	402,000	1,245,100	1,152,700	1,003,200	1,231,700	476,000	353,200	2,258,200	2,540,700	2,433,300
Haleakala NP	480,000	1,561,660	1,372,200	1,196,400	1,196,400	1,404,882	1,458,403	1,492,557	1,533,262	1,551,512
Homestead NM of America	82,000	104,500	104,500	81,198	82,460	82,353	87,731	77,244	114,793	102,939
Hopewell Culture NHP	105,000	95,000	79,322	103,047	99,953	109,519	106,024	106,332	122,874	131,204
Jewel Cave NM	50,000	168,500	168,500	167,140	159,203	153,330	161,422	170,571	170,000	150,000
John Day Fossil Beds NM	95,000	129,000	130,000	115,000	127,101	119,000	129,000	129,000	143,000	122,260
Kalaupapa NHP	211,000	549,000	549,000	549,000	499,000	534,000	549,000	787,000	549,000	549,000
Lake Clark NP and Pr	147,000	321,500	319,810	250,000	262,600	245,800	261,032	259,900	310,000	305,000
Little River Canyon NPr	85,000	182,426	174,027	112,900	171,275	95,898	96,371	111,941	116,000	135,569
Mojave NPr	470,000	1,264,000	1,219,073	1,177,488	1,178,297	1,165,193	1,160,397	1,147,303	1,213,592	1,412,125
Monocacy NB	118,000	120,000	116,000	116,000	116,000	116,000	116,000	116,000	116,000	116,000
Obed Wild and Scenic River	195,000	245,000	193,318	188,775	188,775	188,775	195,000	182,751	195,000	195,000
Padre Island NS[b]	95,000	408,000	403,825	543,000	471,896	600,200	589,492	547,307	809,185	1,671,520
Pictured Rocks NL	55,000	194,650	207,000	211,000	237,000	238,832	243,664	266,547	244,725	224,281
Rock Creek Park	163,000	436,522	393,168	359,104	299,000	376,300	307,977	305,881	392,876	353,103
San Juan Island NHP	95,000	124,600	125,050	124,600	124,600	116,837	101,200	123,230	106,264	105,254
Saugus Iron Works NHS	58,000	58,000	58,000	69,900	58,000	58,000	58,000	58,000	58,000	58,000
Sequoia & Kings Canyon NPs	112,000	1,446,000	1,424,400	1,424,400	1,457,400	1,563,600	1,590,600	1,885,200	1,966,927	1,795,600
Stones River NB	132,000	132,000	137,100	127,924	132,000	208,277	188,182	267,954	476,049	562,177
Sunset Crater, Walnut Canyon, & Wupatki NMs	100,000	166,762	171,227	186,341	191,683	196,426	208,661	204,024	206,917	212,095
Theodore Roosevelt NP	133,000	302,500	292,500	282,500	281,500	264,660	301,400	332,600	383,727	414,392
Virgin Islands NP	399,000	1,077,234	1,002,726	941,500	877,234	877,234	399,000	399,000	399,000	399,000
Zion NP	246,000	536,300	515,872	518,774	485,274	518,774	467,101	492,344	555,828	586,880
TOTAL[a]	6,595,000	17,506,190	16,863,512	16,564,275	17,249,041	16,802,029	16,556,303	19,943,430	21,130,940	22,803,852

[a]FY 2010 report corrects FY 2009 total (corrected from $21,150,940) because FY 2009 figure for Gates of the Arctic was incorrectly reported as $553,000.
[b]FY 2010 total reflects park base increases to improve safety in the natural resource program.

Threatened elkhorn coral (*Acropora palmata*) monitoring plot in Buck Island Reef National Monument in the Virgin Islands. NPS photo.

Appendix B: Natural Resource Program Funding–Servicewide Programs

Table B-1. FY 2010 funding for NPS natural resource programs

Office/program	Total available in FY 2009 ($)	Classified pay increase ($)	Adjustments ($)	Total available in FY 2010 ($)	Change from FY 2009 ($)
Air Quality Program	8,784,000	100,000		8,884,000	100,000
Biological Resource Management Program	9,833,000	136,000		9,969,000	136,000
Climate Change Response Program[a]	0		10,000,000	10,000,000	10,000,000
Cooperative Ecosystem Studies Units[b]	125,000			125,000	0
Geologic Resources Program	3,341,000	79,000		3,420,000	79,000
Inventory and Monitoring Program	45,039,000	456,000		45,495,000	456,000
Natural Resource Data and Information Program	1,911,000	44,000		1,955,000	44,000
Natural Resource Preservation Program	8,099,000			8,099,000	0
Natural Sounds Program	3,545,000	20,000		3,565,000	20,000
Resource Damage Assessment and Restoration Program (including Oil Spill Pollution Act)	1,425,000	28,000		1,453,000	28,000
Resource Protection Fund	283,000			283,000	0
Social Science Program[c]	1,761,000	8,000		1,769,000	8,000
Water Resources Program[d]	12,472,000	148,000	1,250,000	13,870,000	1,398,000

[a]Adjustment reflects funding for new program in FY 2010.
[b]CESU funding listed here is for national network support; see Table B-6 for individual CESU funding.
[c]Total includes Park Use Statistics funding ($282,000).
[d]Adjustment reflects funding for Ocean and Coastal Resources Branch beginning in FY 2010.

Table B-2. Air Quality Program funding by category, FY 2010

Category	FY 2010 funding ($)
Program management and implementation	1,497,000
Air quality monitoring, projects, and analysis	4,832,000
Collaboration and outreach	241,000
Technical assistance	2,314,000
TOTAL	$8,884,000

Table B-3. Biological Resource Management Program funding by category, FY 2010

Category	FY 2010 funding ($)
Biological Resource Management competitive projects in parks	531,500
Ecological restoration	275,000
Endangered species	425,000
Exotic plant management	5,699,000
Highly pathogenic avian influenza	332,000
Integrated pest management	285,000
Invasive animals	285,000
Invasive plants	280,000
Migratory birds	175,000
Operations	493,500
Vegetation mapping	260,000
Wildlife management and health	928,000
Wildlife management and health	925,000
TOTAL	$9,969,000

Table B-4. Climate Change Response Program funding by category, FY 2010

Category	FY 2010 funding ($)
Operations	1,500,000
Enhanced monitoring	3,000,000
Adaptation	5,500,000
TOTAL	$10,000,000

Table B-5. Climate Change Response Program funding for Department of the Interior Landscape Conservation Cooperatives and Climate Science Centers, FY 2010

Unit	FY 2010 funding
Landscape Conservation Cooperatives	
Great Northern	130,000
North Atlantic	260,000
Pacific Islands	130,000
South Atlantic	130,000
Climate Science Centers	
Alaska	130,000
Northwest	130,000
TOTAL	$910,000

Table B-6 Allocation of funding among Cooperative Ecosystem Studies Units, FY 2010

Unit	Fiscal year first funded	FY 2010 funding ($)
Californian[a]	2010	154,000
Chesapeake Watershed	2001	155,000
Colorado Plateau	2001	155,000
Desert Southwest	2001	155,000
Great Basin	2001	155,000
Great Lakes–Northern Forest	2003	155,000
Great Plains	2001	155,000
Great Rivers[a]	2010	154,000
Gulf Coast	2003	155,000
Hawaii-Pacific Islands[a]		
North and West Alaska[a]	2010	154,000
North Atlantic Coast	2001	155,000
Pacific Northwest	2001	155,000
Piedmont–South Atlantic Coast[a]		
Rocky Mountains	2001	155,000
South Florida–Caribbean	2001	155,000
Southern Appalachian Mountains	2001	155,000
TOTAL		$2,322,000

[a]These CESUs were not funded by the Natural Resource Challenge.

Table B-7. Geologic Resources Program funding by category, FY 2010

Category	FY 2010 funding ($)
Cave and karst management	128,000
National Cave and Karst Research Institute	424,000
Coastal geology and engineering	570,000
Disturbed lands restoration/abandoned mineral lands	339,000
Geoscientists-in-the-Parks	246,000
Geologic hazards	80,000
Geologic resource assessment	420,000
Energy and minerals management	704,000
Paleontological resources management	335,000
Soil resources management	174,000
TOTAL	$3,420,000

Table B-8. Inventory and Monitoring Program funding by category, FY 2010

Category	FY 2010 funding ($)
Natural resource inventories	11,067,780
Vital signs monitoring	30,360,075
Information management	1,374,170
Regional coordinators	1,008,300
Program administration	1,684,675
TOTAL	$45,495,000

Table B-9. Allocation of funding among basic natural resource inventories, FY 2010

Category	FY 2010 funding ($)
Air quality related values	160,000
Geologic resources inventories	1,923,000
Soil resources inventories	2,806,300
Alaska vegetation and soil inventories	1,000,000
Paleontology inventories	35,500
Vegetation inventories	4,434,300
Submerged resources inventories	300,000
Species inventories	89,000
Other natural resource inventories	319,680
TOTAL	$11,067,780

Table B-10. Allocation of monitoring funding among Inventory and Monitoring Networks, FY 2010

Network[a]	Fiscal year first funded	Number of parks in network	Water quality monitoring ($)	Vital signs monitoring ($)
Alaska Region				
Arctic	2005	5	144,100	1,622,800
Central Alaska	2002	3	94,200	1,296,800
Southeast Alaska	2006	3	40,400	500,900
Southwest Alaska	2002	5	133,600	1,505,700
Intermountain Region				
Chihuahuan Desert	2007	6	70,200	799,400
Greater Yellowstone	2002	3	68,200	776,100
Northern Colorado Plateau	2002	16	103,700	1,065,100
Rocky Mountain	2004	6	58,600	673,600
Sonoran Desert	2001	11	61,500	729,300
Southern Colorado Plateau	2003	19	119,100	1,278,100
Southern Plains	2006	10	27,900	476,400
Midwest Region				
Great Lakes	2003	9	118,200	1,394,900
Heartland	2001	15	78,800	821,300
Northern Great Plains	2007	13	77,900	962,100
National Capital Region				
National Capital	2002	11	68,200	813,000
Northeast Region				
Eastern Rivers and Mountains	2004	9	60,600	674,800
Mid-Atlantic	2006	10	42,300	375,600
Northeast Coastal and Barrier	2001	8	86,500	797,800
Northeast Temperate	2003	11	57,700	826,400
Pacific West Region				
Klamath	2004	6	73,000	844,900
Mediterranean Coast	2002	3	73,000	340,300
Mojave Desert	2006	6	76,900	920,800
North Coast and Cascades	2001	7	78,800	1,222,800
Pacific Island	2003	9	145,100	1,619,000
San Francisco Bay Area	2002	6	67,200	820,200
Sierra Nevada	2004	3	60,600	695,300
Upper Columbia Basin	2006	8	48,000	561,900
Southeast Region				
Appalachian Highlands	2002	4	67,200	453,500
Cumberland/Piedmont	2001	14	56,700	1,018,200
Gulf Coast	2004	8	85,500	970,900
South Florida/Caribbean	2006	6	141,300	1,602,400
Southeast Coast	2005	17	116,300	1,333,700
Servicewide Data Management				136,600
TOTAL [2]		270	$2,737,900	$29,794,000

[a] Networks are listed by the region that includes the majority of the network area, even though the network may extend into other regions.
[b] Vital signs monitoring funding in this table does not include national program costs; the total, therefore, differs from Table B-8.

Table B-11. Water Resources Program funding by categories, FY 2010

Category	FY 2010 funding ($)
Legacy high-priority projects	182,740
Natural resource condition assessments	2,335,700
Ocean and coastal resources	1,250,000
Water quality vital signs monitoring	2,737,900
Water resource projects	657,800
Water resource protection - aquatic resource professionals	1,327,410
Water resource technical assistance	5,378,450
TOTAL	$13,870,000

Appendix C: Biological Resource Management Competitive Projects

Table C-1. Biological resource projects, FY 2010

Region	State	Park	Project title	FY 2010 funding ($)
AKR	AK	Denali National Park and Preserve	Assessing the impacts of climate change on at-risk boreal forest wetland nesting birds	21,700
	AK	Katmai National Park and Preserve	Assess the status of the harvested brown bear population in Katmai National Preserve	11,200
	AK	Katmai National Park and Preserve	Measuring abundance of kokanee	24,200
IMR	AZ	Saguaro National Park	Test effectiveness of different control methods on invasive buffelgrass	23,900
	CO	Black Canyon of the Gunnison National Monument	Restoring Gunnison grouse habitat as part of Crawford Population recovery effort	23,900
	NM	Carlsbad Caverns National Park	Determine biodiversity patterns of native bee pollinators in the Chihuahuan Desert	25,000
	NM	Guadalupe Mountains National Park	Create experimental colony(ies) of imperiled species of endemic Guadalupe Mountains violet	24,400
	TX	Padre Island National Seashore	Assess impacts of beach recreational activities on endangered shorebirds	33,000
	UT	Bryce Canyon National Park	Utah prairie dog population and habitat conservation plan	25,000
	WY	Yellowstone National Park	Develop techniques to evaluate effectiveness of grizzly bear management areas	17,000
MWR	IN	Indiana Dunes National Lakeshore	Restore endangered Karner blue butterfly to East Unit	11,400
	MI	Isle Royale National Park	Ecological factors affecting extreme genetic and phenotypic diversity in lake trout	24,500
	MI	Pictured Rocks National Lakeshore	Assess interactions of Unionid mussels, yellow perch, and lake trout in Grand Sable Lake	26,700
	WI	Saint Croix National Scenic Riverway	Converting hydropower dam operation to Run-of-the-River: The effect on endangered mussels	16,000
NCR	WV	Chesapeake and Ohio Canal National Historical Park	Radio telemetry survey of small-footed and Indiana Bats at Stickpile and Kessler tunnels	50,000
NER	PA	Valley Forge National Historic Park	Assess genetic distinctiveness of *Cambarus acuminatus*	40,200
	VA	Shenandoah National Park	Control the highly invasive mile-a-minute vine	25,300
PWR	CA	Death Valley National Park	Devils hole physical habitat model	50,000
	WA	Mount Rainier National Park	Protect rare bat colonies	26,000
SER	SC	Congaree National Park	Evaluate dormant season herbicide treatment methods for Chinese privet	32,100
TOTAL				$531,500

Appendix D: Water Resource Program Projects

Table D-1. National Park Service sites with natural resource condition assessment projects in FY 2010 and organization performing the assessments

Region	State	Parks	Agency, cooperator/ partner, or contractor	FY 2010 funding ($)
AKR	AK	Multiple	Pacific Northwest CESU/ Saint Mary's University of Minnesota	149,500
	AK	Yukon-Charley Rivers National Preserve, Sitka National Historical Park	Pacific Northwest CESU/ Saint Mary's University of Minnesota	148,000
IMR	AZ, NM, CO, UT	Multiple	Southern Colorado Plateau Network (project management, contracting, and science support for units on Colorado Plateau)	54,300
	CO	Black Canyon of the Gunnison National Park	Northern Colorado Plateau Network/US Geological Survey	43,000
	CO, AZ, NM	Multiple	Sonoran Desert Network (geospatial products for use in multiple Intermountain Region projects)	50,000
	CO, MT, UT, AZ	Multiple	Rocky Mountain CESU/ Colorado State University (geospatial products for use in multiple Intermountain Region projects)	53,000
	CO, UT	Zion National Park, Curecanti National Recreation Area	Northern Colorado Plateau Network/Colorado Plateau CESU/University of Arizona	106,000
	MT	Bighorn Canyon National Recreation Area	Pacific Northwest Cooperative Ecosystem Studies Unit/Saint Mary's University of Minnesota	35,000
	NM	Bandelier National Monument, Petroglyph National Monument	Southern Colorado Plateau Network (scoping)	7,000
	NM	Capulin Volcano National Monument	Southern Plains Network/ Utah State University/ Colorado State University	32,000
	TX	Big Bend National Park	Pacific Northwest Cooperative Ecosystem Studies Unit/Saint Mary's University of Minnesota	33,000
	Multiple	Multiple	Regional office project support	11,700
MWR	MN, NE, SD, WY	Knife River Indian Villages National Historic Site, Fort Union Trading Post National Historic Site, Theodore Roosevelt National Park	Great Rivers CESU/Saint Mary's University of Minnesota	277,000
NCR	MD, VA	Antietam National Battlefield, Manassas National Battlefield Park, Monocacy National Battlefield (ongoing project)	Chesapeake Watershed CESU/ University of Maryland	50,000
	MD, VA	Catoctin Mountain Park, Chesapeake and Ohio Canal National Historical Park, Harpers Ferry National Historical Park	Chesapeake Watershed CESU/ University of Maryland	24,000

Table D-1 (cont). National Park Service sites with natural resource condition assessment projects in FY 2010 and organization performing the assessments

Region	State	Parks	Agency, cooperator/ partner, or contractor	FY 2010 funding ($)
NER	PA	Allegheny Portage Railroad National Historic Site, Johnstown Flood National Memorial, Fort Necessity National Battlefield, Friendship Hill National Historic Site	Chesapeake Watershed CESU/ University of Maryland	135,000
	VA	Appomattox Court House National Historical Park, Richmond National Battlefield Park (ongoing project)	Southern Appalachian CESU/Virginia Tech	14,600
	Multiple	Multiple	Regional office project support	72,400
PWR	CA	Sequoia and Kings Canyon National Parks (ongoing project)	Californian CESU/University of California, Berkeley	15,000
	CA	Yosemite National Park, Devils Postpile National Monument (ongoing project)	Yosemite National Park	63,500
	CA, OR	Lava Beds National Monument, Lassen Volcanic National Park, Crater Lake National Park	Pacific Northwest CESU/ Southern Oregon University	200,000
	ID, MT	Craters of the Moon National Monument and Preserve, City of Rocks National Reserve, Hagerman Fossil Beds National Monument, Big Hole National Battlefield (ongoing project)	Northwest Management, Inc.	10,000
	WA	Mount Rainier National Park, North Cascades National Park	US Geological Survey-Biological Resources Division–Forest and Rangelands Ecosystem Science Center	115,000
	Multiple	Multiple	Regional office project support	3,500
SER	AL, FL, GA, NC, SC	Chattahoochee River National Recreation Area, Congaree National Park, Kennesaw Mountain National Battlefield Park, Moores Creek National Battlefield, Ocmulgee National Monument, Horseshoe Bend National Military Park, Cape Hatteras National Seashore, Cape Lookout National Seashore, Cumberland Island National Seashore, Timucuan Ecological and Historic National Preserve (ongoing project)	Piedmont–South Atlantic Coast CESU/ North Carolina State University	138,200
	FL	Biscayne National Park	South Florida/Caribbean Network	107,600
	Multiple	Multiple	Regional office project support	50,200
TOTAL				$1,998,500

Table D-2. Water resource protection projects, FY 2010

Region	State	Park	Project title	FY 2010 funding ($)
IMR	CO	Black Canyon of the Gunnison National Park	Data collection and development of a monitoring plan to protect decreed instream flows	15,000
	CO	Great Sand Dunes National Park and Preserve	Hydrogeologic data collection to meet court decree	32,800
	WY	Grand Teton National Park	Development of a water budget for the Gros Ventre River	6,000
PWR	CA, NV	Death Valley National Park	Hydrologic data collection to protect Devils Hole	4,000
	HI	Kaloko-Honokohau National Historical Park, Kalaupapa National Historical Park	Development of a groundwater model and investigation of water-dependent values	276,000
	NV	Great Basin National Park	Hydrologic data collection and groundwater modeling	55,800
	NV	Lake Mead National Recreation Area	Hydrologic data collection and groundwater modeling	15,200
Service-wide		Multiple	Technical support and service to all projects	56,000
		Multiple	Support to the Office of the Solicitor to protect/secure NPS water resources	197,000
TOTAL				$657,800

Table D-3. Ocean and coastal resource project funding, FY 2010

Region	State	Park	Project title	FY 2010 funding ($)
AKR	AK	Glacier Bay National Park and Preserve	Benthic habitat map of West Arm	15,000
	AK	Multiple	Compilation of digital shoreline for Alaska coastal parks	40,000
MWR	MI	Isle Royale National Park	Implement zebra mussel response plan	54,000
NER	MA	Cape Cod National Seashore	Linkages between toxic red tides, hydrodynamics and groundwater nutrient fluxes	243,000
	MD, VA	Assateague Island National Seashore	Inventory benthic habitats and ocean resources	245,000
PWR	CA	Point Reyes National Seashore	Benthic habitat mapping	105,000
	HI	Kaloko-Honokohau National Historical Park, Kalaupapa National Historical Park	Managing ecosystem responses to increasing nutrients	84,000
	WA	San Juan Island National Historical Park	Benthic habitat mapping	52,000
	WA	Olympic National Park	Develop ocean acidification monitoring protocols	54,000
SER	FL	Biscayne National Park	Lionfish eradication	28,000
	FL	Gulf Islands National Seashore	Impacts of Gulf oil spill on submerged aquatic vegetation	19,000
	Multiple	Southeast Regional Office	Integration of water quality and habitat quality data in southeast parks	44,000
TOTAL				$983,000

Table D-4. High-priority water resource project funding, FY 2010

Region	State	Park	Project title	FY 2010 funding ($)
IMR	AZ	Grand Canyon National Park	Develop a water resources information and issues overview report	30,000
	CO	Great Sand Dunes National Park and Preserve	Plug and abandon nine artesian wells	39,700
MWR	AR	Buffalo National River	Zebra Mussel Prevention/Response Plan	50,000
	MI	Isle Royale National Park	Develop and implement Isle Royale National Park Zebra Mussel Response Plan	53,500
	MN, WI	Saint Croix National Scenic Riverway	Assessing pelagic zooplankton in Lake St. Croix in anticipation of invasive Asian carp	22,000
PWR	CA	Sequoia and Kings Canyon National Parks	Halstead Meadow restoration storm repair	25,000
	WA	Olympic National Park	Enhance NPS capacity to monitor ocean acidification	49,500
SER	FL, GA, SC, NC	Multiple	Coastal health of southeast parks: Multi-scale analysis and synthesis	45,000
TOTAL				$314,700

Table D-5. Additional projects funded by the Water Resources Program, FY 2010

Region	State	Park	Project title	FY 2010 funding ($)
IMR	NM	White Sands National Monument	Develop a watershed data inventory for White Sands National Monument and the Tularosa Basin	30,000
	UT	Zion National Park	Virgin River bacterial contamination study	16,300
MWR	SD	Wind Cave National Park	DNA sequencing of species in lakes	20,000
PWR	CA	Death Valley National Park	NPS-USGS inter-agency agreement to process data and develop a monitoring record for the Gravity Fault wells	20,000
	HI	Kaloko-Honokohau National Historical Park	Aimakapa Pond wetland restoration	38,000
	HI	Kaloko-Honokohau National Historical Park	Climate change effects on near-shore marine resources	71,200
	NV	Great Basin National Park	Support for development of the Snake Valley groundwater model	25,000
SER	TN	Obed Wild and Scenic River	Wild and Scenic River Outstanding Resource Values Workshop	14,000
Service-wide	Multiple	Multiple	Acquisition of Aquarius workstation, database, and web portal to manage continuous water resources data	114,000
	Multiple	Multiple	Research associate to support development and delivery of water rights docket information through NRInfo	15,000
	Multiple	Multiple	Amendment to existing NPS-USGS inter-agency agreement for stream gage data processing support (ADAPS)	5,300
TOTAL				$368,800

Appendix E: Climate Change Response Program Projects

Table E-1. Climate Change Response projects, FY 2010

Region	State	Landscape Conservation Cooperative	Park	Project Title	FY 2010 funding ($)
AKR	AK	North Pacific, Western Alaska, Aleutian and Bering Sea Islands, Arctic, Northwestern Interior Forest	Alaska Regional Office	Climate change scenario planning for national parks in Alaska	200,000
IMR	MT	Great Northern	Glacier National Park	Ice patches as sources of archeological and paleoecological data in climate change research	261,000
	Multiple	Great Basin, Southern Rockies, North Pacific	Crater Lake, Lassen Volcanic, Rocky Mountain, Grand Teton, and Yellowstone National Parks; Great Sand Dunes National Park and Preserve; Lava Beds National Monument; Craters of the Moon National Monument and Preserve	Pikas in peril: Multi-regional vulnerability assessment of a climate-sensitive sentinel species	352,000
	Multiple	Every LCC except Pacific Islands, and Peninsular Florida	Yellowstone National Park (lead—75 parks involved)	Multi-regional evaluation of pollinator response to climate change in critical habitats Servicewide	100,000
MWR	SD	Plains and Prairie Potholes	Wind Cave National Park	Quantitative forecasting of above and below ground climate change impacts	73,000
	Multiple	Upper Midwest and Great Lakes	Indiana Dunes National Seashore	Determine the effects of changing climate on the demography of the Karner blue butterfly	101,000
NCR	Multiple	North Atlantic	National Capital Regional Office	Modeling coastal vulnerability for freshwater tidal reaches of the Potomac and Anacostia rivers	145,000
NER	MD, VA	North Atlantic	Assateague Island National Seashore	Improve communication about climate change impacts and park response	134,000
	ME	North Atlantic	Acadia National Park	Inventory and protect salt marshes from risks of sea level rise	50,000
	VA	Appalachian	Shenandoah National Park	Adaptive management, climate change, and endangered species: A case study of Shenandoah salamanders	110,500
PWR	CA	California	Pacific West Regional Office; Golden Gate National Recreation Area; Sequoia and Kings Canyon, Lassen Volcanic, and Joshua Tree National Parks; Redwood National and State Parks; Santa Monica Mountains National Recreation Area	Facilitate phenology network to assess climate change response in California parks	295,000
	CA	California	Yosemite National Park	Impacts of fire management on carbon stock stability in Yosemite, Sequoia, and Kings Canyon National Parks	45,000
	WA	North Pacific	Olympic National Park	Response of Olympic glaciers to climate change	32,000
SER	FL, MS	Gulf Coastal Plains and Ozarks	Gulf Islands National Seashore	Endangered beach mouse: linking population studies/habitat restoration to predicted sea level rise	37,000
	SC	South Atlantic	Congaree National Park	Climate change-induced changes in flow regime, floodplain inundation and species habitats	152,000
Wash. Office	Multiple	South Rockies, Desert, Great Basin	Mojave National Preserve; Grand Canyon, Capitol Reef, Canyonlands, Arches, and Zion National Parks; Glen Canyon and Lake Mead National Recreation Areas	Assessing climate refugia and connectivity for desert bighorn sheep	358,000
	Multiple	Northern Rockies, Southern Rockies	Rocky Mountain, Grand Teton, and Yellowstone National Parks; Great Sand Dunes National Park and Preserve	A cooperative plan for wolverine recovery and management in the conterminous U.S.	228,000
TOTAL					$2,673,500

Table E-2. George Melendez Wright Climate Change Fellowship projects, FY 2010

Region	State	Landscape Conservation Cooperative	Park	Project Title	FY 2010 funding ($)
AKR	AK	Arctic	Noatak National Preserve	Climate change and subsistence fisheries in Noatak, Alaska	19,525
	AK	Great Northern	Glacier National Park	Building knowledge at the landscape scale: Glacier National Park and its neighbors	8,330
	AK	Northwestern Interior Forest	Denali National Park and Preserve	The effects of changing climate on Denali Park glaciers: A case study on the Kahiltna Glacier	17,240
	AK	Northwestern Interior Forest	Yukon Flats Wildlife Refuge	Ecosystem change in boreal wetlands and its relation to wetland birds	19,230
IMR	AZ	Desert	Saguaro National Park	Using historic data to evaluate the effect of climate change on perennial vegetation	9,855
	NM	Desert	Chiricahua National Monument	The indirect effects of climate change: Climate-induced top predator extinctions affect aquatic community structure in arid headwater streams	8,695
	NM	Great Northern	John Day Fossil Beds National Monument	Mammal distribution and niche dynamics in relation to climate change during the Miocene	19,275
	WY, NM	Great Northern, Southern Rockies, Great Basin	Grand Teton National Park, Bandelier National Monument, Great Basin National Park	Long-term vulnerability and risk assessment of a key habitat type throughout the western U.S.: Cottonwood riparian areas	18,195
	Multiple	Great Basin, Southern Rockies, California	Craters of the Moon National Monument and Preserve, Great Sand Dunes National Park and Preserve, Lava Beds National Monument, Rocky Mountain National Park, Yellowstone National Park	Estimating climate-mediated stress in pikas, a sentinel species and key NPS vital sign	19,930
NER	NY, MD, MA, VA	North Atlantic	Cape Cod, Fire Island, and Assateague National Seashores	Salt marsh phenology and productivity in a changing climate	20,000
PWR	CA	California	Golden Gate National Recreation Area	Water relations of *Baccharis pilularis D.C.* seedling establishment in a changing climate	9,050
	CA	California	Lassen Volcanic National Park, Yosemite National Park, and Sequoia and Kings Canyon National Parks	Long-term trends in the avifauna of the Sierra Nevada: Community dynamics in three national parks over a century of climate change	15,520
	CA	California	Point Reyes National Seashore	Impacts of climate change on avian population dynamics: A bottom-up approach	16,000
	CA	California	Point Reyes National Seashore	Climate change vulnerability assessment: Point Reyes National Seashore	13,290
	CA	California	Point Reyes National Seashore	Community responses to global change	11,285
	CA	California	Sequoia and Kings Canyon National Parks	Linking climate change to forest dynamics from seedling- to ecosystem-scales	10,300
	HI	Pacific Islands	Haleakala National Park	Variation in water stress at the upper limit of cloud forest along a secondary climate gradient	19,800
	WA	North Pacific	Mount Rainier National Park	Climate change and range shifts of subalpine and alpine meadows	6,775
	WA	North Pacific	Mount Rainier National Park	Testing the limits: Effects of climate and competition on conifer distributions	6,630
	WA	North Pacific	Olympic National Park	Quantifying shrinking glaciers in Olympic National Park: Impact on summer stream flow	18,058
SER	LA	Gulf Coastal Plains and Ozarks	Jean Lafitte National Historical Park and Preserve	Rainfall events in a hummocky terrain may release saltwater stress of baldcypress (*Taxodium distichum L. Rich*) in the Barataria wetland, Louisiana	6,850
	TN, NC	Appalachian	Great Smoky Mountains National Park	Modeling the past as a window to the future: A study of how climate fluctuations have influenced the distribution and demographic history of the montane salamander, *Plethodon jordani*	15,595
TOTAL					$309,428

Table E-3. George Melendez Wright Climate Change Internship projects, FY 2010

Region	State	Landscape Conservation Cooperative	Park	Project Title	FY 2010 funding ($)
Denver Service Center	CO	Great Northern, North Pacific, Southern Rockies, California	Rocky Mountain National Park, North Cascades National Park, Glacier National Park, Grand Teton National Park, Mount Rainier National Park, Yosemite National Park	Developing a database to ensure the adaptability of native grass seed species for revegetation	6,240
IMR	CO	Southern Rockies	Colorado National Monument	Inventorying / monitoring spring and seep ecosystems and rare plants to help in management decisions and adaptation scenarios	2,814
	CO	Southern Rockies	Rocky Mountain National Park	Collecting data in alpine environments to inform ecological monitoring in this fragile ecosystem	5,760
MWR	MN	Upper Midwest and Great Lakes	Voyageurs National Park	Investigating the temperature tolerance of moose and compare it to existing habitat temperatures in order to estimate their sensitivity to climate change	5,847
NCR	DC	North Atlantic	National Capital Region	Engaging urban youth to address climate change in their communities in collaboration with 2nd Nature program	5,760
NER	ME	North Atlantic	Acadia National Park	Developing a curriculum-based climate change education program, podcast, and other educational and interpretive materials	5,760
	NY	North Atlantic	Fire Island National Seashore	Mapping human-caused barriers to landform migration and developing recommendations to enhance shoreline migration by removing or mitigating structures	5,574
PWR	CA	California	Devils Postpile National Monument	Monitoring lodgepole pines, meadows, cold air pooling, and water flow in the San Joaquin River Valley to build a framework for the park's adaptation strategies	5,418
	OR	North Pacific	Crater Lake National Park	Designing and building a photovoltaic array to showcase sustainable energy throughout the park	5,760
SER	AL	Appalachian	Russell Cave National Monument	Creating interpretive / curriculum-based programs, educating public about prehistoric climate change and comparing it to current and forecasted climatic conditions	5,755
	FL	Peninsular Florida	South Florida/Caribbean Network	Monitoring mangrove and colonial bird nesting to assess threat of sea level rise	7,680
	TN, NC	Appalachian	Great Smoky Mountains National Park	Developing education products for a high school students (movie, citizen science field lesson, and an interactive on-line activities)	6,030
Wash. Office	Multiple	Southern Rockies	Yellowstone National Park, Grand Canyon National Park, El Malpais National Monument	Developing climate change adaptation policy and evaluating proposed wilderness areas for future migration corridors and refugia	8,253
TOTAL					$76,651

Table E-4. Additional projects funded by the Climate Change Response Program, FY 2010

Region	State	Landscape Conservation Cooperative	Park	Project Title	FY 2010 funding ($)
AKR	AK	Northwestern Interior Forest, Western Alaska	AKR Regional Office, Katmai National Park and Preserve, Lake Clark National Park and Preserve	Understanding 8,000 years of climate change through archeofaunal analyses, SW Alaska	126,000
NCR	DC, MD, VA, WV	Appalachian, North Atlantic, South Atlantic	National Capital Regional Office	Framework for a vulnerability assessment of forest birds in the National Capital Region	104,000
NER	ME	North Atlantic	Acadia National Park	Seabird study	100,000
	Multiple	North Atlantic	Eastern Rivers and Mountains I&M Network	Develop water quality monitoring for climate change	31,300
PWR	HI	Pacific Islands	Multiple Hawaiian Parks	Designing a framework to address climate impacts on cultural resources	75,000
SER	FL	Peninsular Florida	Canaveral National Seashore	Oyster mapping: Mapping impacts of recreational boating vs restoration on oyster reefs (ongoing project)	130,000
TOTAL					$566,300

Appendix F: Resource Protection (RP) Projects

Table F-1. Resource Protection fully funded projects, FY 2010

Region	State	Park	Project title	FY 2010 funding ($)
IMR	WY	Grand Teton National Park	Protect bears and other wildlife with new VIP brigade, protocols, and media	39,000
MWR	MO	Ozark National Scenic Riverways	Protect natural and cultural resources from illegal off-road vehicle impacts	76,000
TOTAL				$115,000

Table F-2. Resource Protection new and ongoing projects, FY 2010

Region	State	Park	Project title	FY 2010 funding ($)
AKR	AK	Glacier Bay National Park and Preserve	Protect bears from human-caused mortalities, disturbance, and displacement	27,000
IMR	AZ	Petrified Forest National Park	Inventory and protect critical natural resources on expansion lands	24,000
PWR	CA	Point Reyes National Seashore	Nip marijuana cultivation in the bud to prevent cultivation on park lands through early detection	29,000
SER	KY	Mammoth Cave National Park	Protecting and preserving poached plant communities	38,000
	LA	Jean Lafitte National Historical Park and Preserve	Enhance natural resource protection by using remote surveillance systems	50,000
TOTAL				$168,000

Appendix G: Natural Resource Preservation Program (NRPP) Projects

Table G-1. NRPP–Alaska Special Projects, FY 2010

Park	Project title	FY 2010 funding ($)
Denali National Park and Preserve	Design and test survey techniques to estimate Dall's sheep abundance in Alaskan parks	24,650
Denali National Park and Preserve	Inventory the bryophyte and lichen flora of Denali, Yukon-Charley, and Wrangell-St. Elias	16,205
Denali National Park and Preserve	Modeling caribou habitat at a landscape scale to determine the potential impacts of climate change	31,333
Denali National Park and Preserve	Monitor subsistence fisheries throughout the northwest portion of Denali National Park	22,649
Denali National Park and Preserve	Quantifying abundance and distribution of breeding trumpeter swan population	11,378
Kenai Fjords National Park	Assess abundance, distribution, and reproductive status of peregrine falcons	52,296
Kenai Fjords National Park	Quantify thickness of Harding Icefield	86,330
Lake Clark National Park and Preserve	Assess wolf population status and predation rate	67,395
Wrangell-St. Elias National Park and Preserve	Burbot stock assessment in Tanada Lake and Copper Lake	62,100
Yukon-Charley Rivers National Preserve	Cretaceous Alaska: Paleontological inventory of Yukon-Charley Rivers National Preserve	52,621
Yukon-Charley Rivers National Preserve	Understanding lake disappearance through time in northern Alaskan parks	35,373
Other		4,670
TOTAL		$467,000

Table G-2. NRPP–Disturbed Lands Restoration fully funded projects, FY 2010

Region	State	Park	Project title	FY 2010 funding ($)
IMR	MT	Glacier National Park	Restoration of soils and vegetation at Running Eagle Falls	10,000
	TX	Lyndon B. Johnson National Historical Park	Restore prairie at five national park units in three states	48,000
NCR	VA	Prince William Forest Park	Disturbed land restoration of the headwaters of Quantico Creek	8,000
PWR	CA	Point Reyes National Seashore	Restoring historic rock quarries	13,000
	CA	Redwood National and State Parks	Strawberry Creek collaborative watershed restoration	133,000
SER	GA	Chattahoochee River National Recreation Area	Support corporate wetland restoration partnership initiative in Johnson Ferry Unit	24,000
	LA	Jean Lafitte National Historical Park and Preserve	Restore 15 miles of oil and gas canals to natural landscape	101,000
TOTAL				$337,000

Table G-3. NRPP–Disturbed Lands Restoration new and ongoing projects, FY 2010

Region	State	Park	Project title	FY 2010 funding ($)
IMR	MT	Glacier National Park	Stabilization of eroding soils and restoration of vegetation to the Big Bend Area	20,000
	AZ	Grand Canyon National Park	Restore disturbed habitat of threatened and endangered sentry milk-vetch, a Grand Canyon endemic	28,000
	WY	Grand Teton National Park	Restore ecological processes and native vegetation to the former Flagg Ranch site	87,000
PWR	CA	Whiskeytown National Recreation Area	Restore geomorphology of Paige-Boulder watershed to reestablish habitat for T&E species	145,000
	CA	Sequoia and Kings Canyon National Park	Restore critical wetlands in Lower Halstead Meadow crossed by the primary park Generals Highway	173,000
TOTAL				$453,000

Table G-4. NRPP–Natural Resource Management fully funded projects FY 2010

Region	State	Park	Project title	FY 2010 funding ($)
IMR	AZ	Canyon de Chelly National Monument	Implement restoration prescriptions: Native seed collection, propagation and revegetation	124,000
	CO	Curecanti National Recreation Area	Purchase self-contained, high-pressure boat wash station to prevent invasive mussel infestation	206,000
	CO	Rocky Mountain National Park	Reduce elk numbers to restore a healthy ecosystem that supports diverse wildlife	117,000
	MT, WY	Yellowstone National Park	Management of introduced mountain goats in Yellowstone	81,000
MWR	SD	Badlands National Park	Assess long-term viability of swift fox in Badlands NP and South Dakota	96,000
	IN	Indiana Dunes National Lakeshore	Restore the biological resources of the Cowles Bog Wetland Complex: Phase II–fen recovery	67,000
	MN	Voyageurs National Park	Assessing the effects of the Namakan Reservoir operations on lake sturgeon ecological habitats	89,000
	Multiple	Midwest Regional Office	Determine invasion status and ecological impacts of an exotic zooplankter in Great Lakes parks	35,000
	Multiple	Midwest Regional Office	Risk of plague to prairie dog populations in five Great Plains parks	47,000
NER	MA	Boston Harbor Islands National Recreation Area	Sediment transport and salt marsh development	164,000
	MA	Cape Cod National Seashore	Cape Cod shoreline change and resource protection	54,000
PWR	CA	Channel Islands National Park	Eradicate dense fennel and facilitate eradication of feral pigs	90,000
	WA	North Cascades National Park	Eradicate non-native trout from seven lakes	107,000
TOTAL				$1,277,000

Table G-5. NRPP–Natural Resource Management new and ongoing projects, FY 2010

Region	State	Park	Project title	FY 2010 funding ($)
AKR	AK	Glacier Bay National Park and Preserve	Determine impacts of increased cruise ship traffic on endangered humpback whales	67,000
	AK	Wrangell-St. Elias National Park and Preserve	Understanding population declines of Kittlitz's murrelet in Icy Bay, Wrangell-St. Elias NP	161,000
IMR	AZ	Organ Pipe Cactus National Monument	Illegal migration in Arizona border parks: assessment, protection, and restoration of resources	166,000
	AZ	Saguaro National Park	Restore native saguaro community following removal of invasives	70,000
	NM	Bandelier National Monument	Restore degraded pinon-juniper landscape PART 1	127,000
	TX	Amistad National Recreation Area	Survey and monument 36 miles of impacted park boundary	39,000
MWR	MI	Sleeping Bear Dunes National Lakeshore	Identify the sources, species and pathways in recent type E botulism waterfowl dieoffs within Sleeping Bear Dunes	50,000
	SD	Badlands National Park	Determine erosion rates at select fossil sites to develop a paleontological monitoring program	96,000
NCR	Multiple	National Capital Regional Office	Detecting and mapping new invasive species occurrences	20,000
NER	NY	Fire Island National Seashore	Restoration of bayside sediment processes	28,000
	WV	New River Gorge National River	Inventory and assess cliff resources and visitor use	100,000
PWR	CA	Channel Islands National Park	Eradicate alien Argentine ants on Santa Cruz Island	47,000
	CA	Pinnacles National Monument	Restore rare bottomlands of newly acquired ranch	63,000
	CA	Pinnacles National Monument	Protect recently acquired sensitive new lands from exotic pigs	97,000
	CA	Point Reyes National Seashore	Marine resource assessment for marine protected areas	61,000
	CA	Point Reyes National Seashore	Stop Scotch broom invasion into wilderness and high-priority areas	80,000
	CA	Santa Monica Mountains National Recreation Area	Sources, prevalence, and impacts of anticoagulant poisons	57,000
	WA	Olympic National Park	Understanding trends of sport fishing on critical fishery Resources	89,000
SER	FL	Dry Tortugas National Park	Dry Tortugas research natural area implementation	94,000
	NC	Blue Ridge Parkway	Develop wetlands mgmt plan and implement adaptive mgmt on Blue Ridge Parkway wetlands	99,000
	NC, TN	Great Smoky Mountains National Park	Saving the Smoky Mountain hemlock forests from destruction by an exotic invasive insect	116,000
Wash. Office	Multiple	Air Quality - Washington Office	Complete night sky assessments in Class I parks and initiate monitoring	135,000
TOTAL				$1,862,000

Table G-6. NRPP–Regional Program Block Allocation projects, FY 2010

Region	State	Park	Project title	FY 2010 funding ($)
AKR	AK	Alaska Regional Office	Alaska scientific and technical reports	5,877
	AK	Alaska Regional Office	Coastal Alaska Park Science Symposium 2010	24,965
	AK	Alaska Regional Office	Coastal Alaska Park Science Symposium 2010	24,965
	AK	Alaska Regional Office	Complete production of NPS Alaska Region satellite image map series	20,385
	AK	Alaska Regional Office	Implement social science strategy for research in Alaska	5,877
	AK	Alaska Regional Office	Natural resource employees professionalization and technical competency enhancement	19,590
	AK	Alaska Regional Office	Produce *Alaska Park Science* journal	36,360
	AK	Denali National Park and Preserve	Documenting traplines and trapping activities in two Alaska parks	42,434
	AK	Denali National Park and Preserve	Implement regional integrated pest management (IPM) program to insure health of natural resources	4,677
IMR	AZ	Pipe Spring National Monument	Implement cooperative study to understand bat ecology of Pipe Spring NM and the Kaibab Paiute Reservation	20,000
	AZ	Tumacacori National Monument	Remove invasive exotic plants from riparian habitat at Tumacacori	20,000
	AZ, UT	Glen Canyon National Recreation Area	Monitor remnant terrace erosion between Glen Canyon Dam and Lees Ferry	20,000
	TX	Amistad National Recreation Area	Determine breeding success of interior least terns on islands within Lake Amistad Reservoir	20,000
	UT	Bryce Canyon National Park	Implement exotic plant control to areas identified through inventories	19,900
	UT	Timpanogos Cave National Monument	Restore cave resources	20,000
MWR	IA	Effigy Mounds National Monument	Control and survey new garlic mustard populations	7,125
	IA	Herbert Hoover National Historic Site	Prevent the loss of prairie restoration area to exotic/invasive plant incursion	9,800
	MI	Isle Royale National Park	Assessing exposure to epizootics and contaminants by determining migration routes of the common loon	17,575
	MI	Sleeping Bear Dunes National Lakeshore	Identify the sources, species and pathways in recent type E botulism waterfowl dieoffs within Sleeping Bear Dunes	15,010
	MN, WI	Saint Croix National Scenic Riverway	Conduct aquatic plant survey within the St. Croix National Scenic Riverway	17,765
	MN, WI	Saint Croix National Scenic Riverway	Restore fish habitat in the cold water zone of the Namekagon River	3,500
	MO	Ozark National Scenic Riverways	Viewshed analysis at Ozark National Scenic Riverways	17,575
MWR	MT, ND	Fort Union Trading Post National Historic Site	Develop reconstructed prairie vegetation management plan	17,575
	ND	Theodore Roosevelt National Park	Treat aggressive exotic species in northern Great Plains parks to restore native plant communities	19,840
	SD	Badlands National Park	Expand park paleontological database to cover all of the fossil exhibit trail area	17,575
	SD	Jewel Cave National Monument	Develop cave rescue operation procedures	17,575
	WI	Apostle Islands National Lakeshore	Determine changes in Apostle Island wetlands due to climate change and invasive species	17,575

Table G-6 (cont). NRPP–Regional Program Block projects, FY 2010

Region	State	Park	Project title	FY 2010 funding ($)
NCR	DC	Rock Creek Park	Where are the flying squirrels	2,000
	MD	Catoctin Mountain Park	Expand access to Catoctin Mountain Park natural resource information	9,200
	MD, VA	George Washington Memorial Parkway	Beetle survey of the George Washington Memorial Parkway (Insecta: Coleoptera)	20,000
	WV	Harpers Ferry National Historical Park	Inventory of park vascular plants – phase I – Maryland Heights	12,000
	Multiple	National Capital Regional Office	Estimating the potential for seedling regeneration in forests of NCR	17,800
	Multiple	National Capital Regional Office	Integrating science with resource management through collaborative approaches	25,000
	Multiple	National Capital Regional Office	Photo-interpretation and accuracy assessment for vegetation classification in NCR	25,000
	Multiple	National Capital Regional Office	Providing opportunities for profession development for NCR natural resource	25,000
	Multiple	National Capital Regional Office	Remove invasive exotic microstegium stiltgrass from critical habitats	25,000
	Multiple	National Capital Regional Office	Supporting science-informed decision making in NCR parks	25,000
NER	MA	Boston Harbor Islands National Recreation Area	Restore natural biodiversity to Boston Harbor Islands	17,580
	MA	Cape Cod National Seashore	Prepare environmental impact statement for the estuarine restoration of Herring River	14,400
	ME	Acadia National Park	Develop restoration prescriptions for impaired streams	10,700
	NY	Fire Island National Seashore	Development of a vegetation management plan	45,000
	NY, PA	Upper Delaware Scenic and Recreational River	Determine age structure of American shad in the Upper Delaware River	12,491
	PA	Valley Forge National Historical Park	An evaluation of existing vegetation data and data gaps leading to inventories and forest management	28,823
	PA, NJ	Delaware Water Gap National Recreation Area	Control alien invasive common reed in wetlands	11,500
	VA	Richmond National Battlefield Park	Remove invasive exotics from ten acres of old growth forest at Gaines' Mill Unit	17,352
NER	VA	Shenandoah National Park	Eradicate wavyleaf basketgrass	15,727
	VA	Shenandoah National Park	Status and trends of park fisheries–a pilot initiative for reporting monitoring information	6,177
PWR	CA	Mojave National Preserve	Genetic analysis of hybridization between Mohave tui and Arroyo chubs	30,000
	CA	Sequoia and Kings Canyon National Park	Determining optimal planting densities for the restoration of Halstead Meadow	50,000
	CA	Sequoia and Kings Canyon National Park	Restoration of mountain yellow-legged frogs and high mountain lakes and streams	24,910
	CA	Sequoia and Kings Canyon National Park	Restore reed canarygrass-invaded meadows in Grant Grove	36,223
	CA	Whiskeytown National Recreation Area	Conduct pre- and post-restoration monitoring (hydrologic, geochemical, and vegetation) for *Puccinelli*	8,000
	HI	Hawaii Volcanoes National Park	Begin recovery of endangered *Cyanea shipmanii*	6,310
	WA	Olympic National Park	Improve razor clam management at Olympic National Park by predicting pathogen outbreaks	20,557
	Multiple	Pacific West Regional Office	Regionwide planning for vertebrate diversity resurvey in Great Basin and Mojave parks	10,000

Table G-6 (cont). NRPP–Regional Program Block projects, FY 2010

Region	State	Park	Project title	FY 2010 funding ($)
SER	FL	Canaveral National Seashore	Assess importance of freshwater wetlands to amphibian and reptile biodiversity	15,000
	FL, MS	Gulf Islands National Seashore	Determine population status of newly discovered bee species and identify habitat conservation needs	25,000
	GA	Cumberland Island National Seashore	Plug or cap abandoned artesian water wells on Cumberland Island	21,000
	KY, TN	Big South Fork National River and Recreation Area	River habitat mapping (bathymetric) for pools, riffles, and endangered species mussel habitat	25,000
	KY, TN, VA	Cumberland Gap National Historical Park	Vegetation survey of cliff systems	25,000
	LA	Jean Lafitte National Historical Park and Preserve	Re-survey small mammals to document changes in rare and exotic species at the Barataria Preserve	23,000
	NC, TN	Great Smoky Mountains National Park	Restore damaged streambank and wetland in agricultural lease	25,000
	SC	Congaree National Park	Eradicate two new exotic wisteria infestations	25,000
Other				83,730
TOTAL				$1,303,000

Table G-7. NRPP–Regional Small Park Block Allocation projects, FY 2010

Region	State	Park	Project title	FY 2010 funding ($)
AKR	AK	Klondike Gold Rush National Historical Park	Monitoring air quality in the Southeast Alaska Network: Linking pollutants with ecological effects	9,405
	AK	Sitka National Historical Park	Conduct benthic invertebrate and algae investigations to determine biological water quality indexes	9,405
IMR	AZ	Casa Grande Ruins National Monument	Integrated pest management program	19,900
	AZ	Fort Bowie National Historic Site	Apache Spring watershed soil loss reduction and reversal	20,000
	AZ	Pipe Spring National Monument	Monitor groundwater levels for hydrogeologic study of Pipe Spring	36,000
	CO	Colorado National Monument	Restore native vegetation after resurfacing historic Rim Rock Drive	9,980
	CO	Florissant Fossil Beds National Monument	Invasive weed control and riparian area restoration	20,000
	NM	Chaco Culture National Historical Park	Survey, assess condition, and map paleontological resources in Clys Canyon and Mockingbird areas	19,700
	NM	Pecos National Historical Park	Remove/replace exotic flora (Siberian elm) endangering historic trading post building	20,000
	OK	Chickasaw National Recreation Area	Install gauging station to protect water rights for historic spring district	20,000
	TX	San Antonio Missions National Historical Park	Assess sustainability of state-threatened reptiles	20,000
	UT	Arches National Park	Assessing ecological impacts of tamarisk leaf beetle on treated tamarisk stands	20,000
	UT	Natural Bridges National Monument	Evaluate status and trends of sensitive plant species in seeps and springs	20,000
	UT	Timpanogos Cave National Monument	Restore lower passage environment of Timpanogos Cave	20,000
	Multiple	Intermountain Regional Office	Create exotic vegetation management plans–Fossil Butte NM and Golden Spike NHS	10,000
MWR	AR	Arkansas Post National Memorial	Native plant restoration through exotic plant control	15,010
	IA	Herbert Hoover National Historic Site	Remove 15 acres of exotic plant infestation in restored prairie and return biodiversity to area	14,575
	MN	Grand Portage National Monument	Ethnobotanical plant restoration	18,010
	MN	Pipestone National Monument	Inventory riparian areas and implement disturbed lands restoration	13,405
	MT, ND	Fort Union Trading Post National Historic Site	Develop reconstructed prairie vegetation management plan	3,000
	MT, ND	Fort Union Trading Post National Historic Site	Initiate integrated resource implementation plan development	9,810
	ND	Theodore Roosevelt National Park	Treat aggressive exotic species in northern Great Plains parks to restore native plant communities	31,200
MWR	NE	Homestead National Monument of America	Restoring the lowland bur oak community, a critically impaired community type	15,010
	SD	Mount Rushmore National Memorial	Conduct survey of two extremely rare terrestrial snails	10,010
	SD	Mount Rushmore National Memorial	Response of plant and small mammal communities to thinning/prescribed fire in mature forests	30,010
	Multiple	Midwest Regional Office	MWR Science Strategy support	1,460
NCR	MD	Antietam National Battlefield	Restoration and rehabilitation of riparian buffers along Antietam and Sharpsburg creeks	14,000

Table G-7 (cont). NRPP–Regional Small Park Block projects, FY 2010

Region	State	Park	Project title	FY 2010 funding ($)
	MD, VA	George Washington Memorial Parkway	Revegetation of Roaches Run eastern shore	3,000
	Multiple	National Capital Regional Office	Estimating the potential for seedling regeneration in forests of NCR	2,000
NER	MA	Boston Harbor Islands National Recreation Area	Determine bat community composition of six northeast parks	55,000
	MA	Boston Harbor Islands National Recreation Area	Restore natural biodiversity to Boston Harbor Islands	2,420
	VA	Colonial National Historical Park	Control phragmites through aerial and ground spraying	13,251
	VA	Richmond National Battlefield Park	Conduct biological inventories at newly acquired park sites	7,169
	VA	Valley Forge National Historical Park	Resource Stewardship Strategy	20,000
	Multiple	Northeast Regional Director's Staff	Develop a volunteer-based bird monitoring protocol for small parks	17,000
PWR	American Samoa	National Park of American Samoa	Reduce and control the most destructive invasive tree in NPSA: *Falcataria moluccana*	26,608
	American Samoa	National Park of American Samoa	Reduce feral pigs in a manner that will attract village participation	27,100
	AZ	Grand Canyon-Parashant National Monument	Baseline inventory and documentation of cave and karst resources	28,495
	CA	Lava Beds National Monument	Analyze perennial ice resources within lava tubes	5,020
	CA	Lava Beds National Monument	Replace old trail/cave counters with TRAFx Advanced Counting Systems	3,637
	Guam	War in the Pacific National Historical Park	Assessing diverse visitation and mitigating potential impacts to park coral reefs	25,540
	ID	Craters of the Moon National Monument and Preserve	Complete exotic plant management plan and environmental compliance for five small park units	26,700
	OR, WA	Lewis and Clark National Historical Park	Restoration of recently acquired coastal forest and dunes	17,900
SER	GA	Chattahoochee River National Recreation Area	Assessment of riparian conditions	25,000
	GA	Ocmulgee National Monument	Eradicate exotic fauna	15,000
	NC	Carl Sandburg Home National Historic Site	Manage invasive exotic plants and insects and monitor natural resources	22,000
	SC	Kings Mountain National Military Park	Monitor invasive exotic plant populations and retreat resprouts	25,000
	TN	Obed Wild and Scenic River	Early detection of hemlock wooly adelgid	25,000
	TN	Stones River National Battlefield	Creating a more sustainable landscape: Crop field conversion	19,900
	Multiple	Southeast Regional Office	Invasive plant control SE-EPMT Asheville Corridor	25,000
	Multiple	Southeast Regional Office	Natural resource workshop for SER parks	25,000
Other				20,370
TOTAL				$933,000

Table G-8. NRPP–Servicewide projects, FY 2010

Park	Project title	FY 2010 funding ($)
Associate Director, NRSS	Director's annual natural resource awards	20,500
Associate Director, NRSS	George Wright Society Biennial Conference Support	75,000
Associate Director, NRSS	Graphic design and web development to support NRPC and NRSS	24,000
Associate Director, NRSS	Herbarium imaging project	40,600
Associate Director, NRSS	Integration of I&M products in ORV stabilization and construction	20,000
Associate Director, NRSS	National coordination support for Research Learning Centers	16,000
Associate Director, NRSS	National Council for Science and the Environment conference support	5,000
Associate Director, NRSS	Park Science Bulletin FY 2010	20,000
Associate Director, NRSS	Provide contracted software engineering services (STAR and PUPS)	20,000
Associate Director, NRSS	Upgrade Report to Congress	7,500
NRSS Air Quality Program	Assessing risk to resources in the Four Corners area from excess nitrogen deposition	63,000
NRSS Biological Resource Management Division	Biscayne National Park BioBlitz and ATBI events support	100,000
NRSS Biological Resource Management Division	Blue Ribbon Panel/Wildlife Society	6,700
NRSS Biological Resource Management Division	Buffelgrass project (Saguaro NP)	50,000
NRSS Biological Resource Management Division	First annual all taxa biotic inventory	2,500
NRSS Biological Resource Management Division	Partners in Flight, International Migratory Bird Day, and Conservation Biology/Wildlife Society	30,000
NRSS Biological Resource Management Division	Wolverine restoration: Northern Rockies LCC, multi-state, and NGO collaboration	78,000
NRSS Geologic Resources Division	Coastal geology expertise to support MSCIP Barrier Island Restoration Supplemental EIS at Gulf Islands NS	22,000
NRSS Geologic Resources Division	Convene an energy strategy session	15,000
NRSS Geologic Resources Division	Develop education and outreach materials for and support research and field surveys of fossils	30,000
NRSS Geologic Resources Division	Monitor fossils and develop monitoring prescriptions at Arches National Park, Death Valley National Park, Glen Canyon National Recreation Area, and Montezuma Castle National Monument	55,000
NRSS Water Quality Division	Aquatic and marine invasive species	45,000
TOTAL		$745,800

Table G-9. NRPP–Threatened and Endangered Species fully funded projects, FY 2010

Region	State	Park	Project title	FY 2010 funding ($)
IMR	TX	Padre Island National Seashore	Establish new techniques to protect increasing numbers of endangered Kemp's ridley sea turtle eggs	46,000
MWR	MN, WI	Saint Croix National Scenic Riverway	Modeling sediment dynamics in the St. Croix River and the impact on federally endangered mussels	50,000
SER	NC, TN	Great Smoky Mountains National Park	Recovery evaluation of introduced endangered and threatened fish species	24,000
TOTAL				$120,000

Table G-10. NRPP–Threatened and Endangered Species new and ongoing projects, FY 2010

Region	State	Park	Project title	FY 20010 funding ($)
IMR	AZ, UT	Glen Canyon National Recreation Area	Create a protected nursery to expand populations of endangered Colorado River native fish	11,000
	CO	Rocky Mountain National Park	Determine the distribution of greenback cutthroat trout	51,000
	MT	Glacier National Park	Preservation of threatened bull trout	50,000
	NM	Carlsbad Caverns National Park	Perform baseline survey and habitat model validation for threatened Mexican spotted owls	64,000
	TX	Big Bend National Park	Protect threatened Chisos hedgehog cactus from exotic grass invasion	34,000
MWR	MO	Ozark National Scenic Riverways	Determine summer habitat use by Indiana bats to inform adaptive management actions	39,000
NCR	VA	Prince William Forest Park	Restore the federally threatened small-whorled pogonia in three NPS regions	37,000
PWR	CA	Golden Gate National Recreation Area	Enhance habitat for GGNRA mission blue butterfly through habitat disturbance actions	42,000
	CA	Pinnacles National Monument	Restoring California condors at Pinnacles NM: Use of isotopes to identify sources of lead poisoning	5,000
SER	NC, TN	Great Smoky Mountains National Park	Determine habitat requirements and survey for federally endangered spruce-fir moss spider	14,000
TOTAL				$347,000

Appendix H: Park-Oriented Biological Support (POBS) Projects

Table H-1. Park-Oriented Biological Support (POBS) Projects, FY 2010

Region	State	Park	Project title
IMR	CO	Rocky Mountain National Park	Developing a non-invasive technique for bighorn sheep population estimation using fecal DNA, Rocky Mountain National Park
	ID	City of Rocks National Reserve	Vegetation and fire history of City of Rocks (CIRO) National Reserve: Relevance for understanding the role of climate and disturbance in plant migration in the American West[a]
	MT	Glacier National Park	Assessing the threat of climate change to headwater amphibians in Glacier National Park
	MT	Glacier National Park	Maximizing legacy databases to understand climate change effects on alpine vegetation[a]
	TX	Padre Island National Seashore	Ecological importance of biodiversity hotspots to coastal sharks: Characterizing apex predator usage of Padre Island National Seashore
MWR	MI	Sleeping Bear Dunes National Lakeshore	Algal benthic invertebrate community as a source of bird botulism pathogen
	NE	Niobrara National Scenic River	Past and present tree density in Niobrara Valley forest: Implications for managing paper birch populations
	OH	Cuyahoga Valley National Park	Implementation of models for predicting exceedances of *E. coli* standards in the Cuyahoga River, Cuyahoga Valley National Park, Ohio
	SD	Badlands National Park	Pollination webs to guide management of rare and invasive species in a changing climate
PWR	CA	Channel Islands National Park	Channel Islands loggerhead shrike population size and territory locations
	CA	Sequoia and Kings Canyon National Parks	Designing a giant sequoia monitoring program
	CA	Yosemite National Park, Sequoia and Kings Canyon National Parks	Integrating early detection and control of velvetgrass (*Holcus lanatus*) in Yosemite and Sequoia-Kings National Parks
	CA	Yosemite National Park	The effects of fire severity on California spotted owl habitat use in a burned landscape in Yosemite National Park, California
	CA	Yosemite National Park, Lassen Volcanic National Park, Sequoia and Kings Canyon National Parks, Devils Postpile National Monument	Impact of climate change on future suitability of the Sierra Nevada for wolverines[a]
	HI	Haleakala National Park	Population dynamics and pollination ecology of the threatened Haleakala silversword
	WA	Olympic National Park	Evaluate fisher restoration in Olympic National Park
SER	FL	Dry Tortugas National Park	Human fecal microflora as a source of coral pathogens in the Dry Tortugas National Park: Are coral pathogens invasives or endemic
	LA	Jean Lafitte National Historical Park and Preserve	Effects of dredge spoil applications on subsiding coastal bald cypress swamps in Jean Lafitte National Historical Park and Preserve
	NC, TN	Great Smoky Mountains National Park	Identifying the appropriate unit of management for GRSM brook trout (*Salvelinus fontinalis*)
	Virgin Islands	Virgin Islands National Park	Exploring the links between coral reefs and mangroves: Characterization of Hurricane Hole, Virgin Islands Coral Reef National Monument[a]

[a]Project received climate change funding.

Park Index

A

Acadia National Park 14, 39, 42, 57, 68, 70, 71, 77
Allegheny Portage Railroad National Historic Site 39, 65
Amistad National Recreation Area 75, 76
Antietam National Battlefield 36, 57, 64, 79
Apostle Islands National Lakeshore 3, 33, 54, 76
Appalachian National Scenic Trail 39, 42, 57
Appomattox Court House National Historical Park 40, 65
Arches National Park 29, 68, 79, 81
Arkansas Post National Memorial 79
Assateague Island National Seashore 40, 66, 69, 68

B

Badlands National Park 1, 22, 33, 74, 75, 76, 83
Bandelier National Monument 14, 64, 69, 75
Bent's Old Fort National Historic Site 29
Big Bend National Park 64, 82
Big Cypress National Preserve 57
Big Hole National Battlefield 65
Bighorn Canyon National Recreation Area 64
Big South Fork National River and Recreation Area 16, 78
Biscayne National Park 15, 18, 22, 48, 49, 53, 65, 66, 81
Black Canyon of the Gunnison National Park 63, 64, 66
Blue Ridge Parkway 48, 75
Booker T. Washington National Monument 40
Boston Harbor Islands National Recreation Area 40, 42, 54, 74, 77, 80
Bryce Canyon National Park 63, 76
Buck Island Reef National Monument 48, 57
Buffalo National River 67

C

Canaveral National Seashore 48, 71, 78
Canyon de Chelly National Monument 74
Canyonlands National Park 68
Cape Cod National Seashore 19, 40, 66, 69, 74, 77
Cape Hatteras National Seashore 65
Cape Krusenstern National Monument 25
Cape Lookout National Seashore 48, 54, 65
Capitol Reef National Park 68
Capulin Volcano National Monument 64
Carl Sandburg Home National Historic Site 80

Carlsbad Caverns National Park 63, 82
Casa Grande Ruins National Monument 29, 79
Catoctin Mountain Park 8, 36, 57, 64, 77
Chaco Culture National Historical Park 79
Channel Islands National Park 43, 54, 57, 74, 75, 83
Chattahoochee River National Recreation Area 49, 65, 73, 80
Chesapeake and Ohio Canal National Historical Park 36, 37, 63, 64
Chickasaw National Recreation Area 29, 79
Chiricahua National Monument 30, 69
City of Rocks National Reserve 43, 65, 83
Colonial National Historical Park 80
Colorado National Monument 70, 79
Congaree National Park 63, 65, 68, 78
Coronado National Memorial 57
Crater Lake National Park 65, 70
Craters of the Moon National Monument and Preserve 7, 65, 68, 69, 80
Cumberland Gap National Historical Park 78
Cumberland Island National Seashore 49, 65, 78
Curecanti National Recreation Area 29, 57, 64, 74

D

Death Valley National Park 63, 66, 67, 81
Delaware Water Gap National Recreation Area 41, 77
Denali National Park and Preserve 25, 27, 63, 69, 73, 76
Devils Postpile National Monument 65, 70, 83
Dinosaur National Monument 30, 57
Dry Tortugas National Park 49, 75, 83

E

Effigy Mounds National Monument 76
El Malpais National Monument 70

F

Fire Island National Seashore 54, 69, 70, 75, 77
Florissant Fossil Beds National Monument 79
Fort Bowie National Historic Site 79
Fort Necessity National Battlefield 65
Fort Union Trading Post National Historic Site 64, 76, 79
Fredericksburg and Spotsylvania National Military Park 40
Friendship Hill National Historic Site 65

G

Gates of the Arctic National Park and Preserve 26, 57
Gateway National Recreation Area 41
George Washington Birthplace National Monument 17
George Washington Memorial Parkway 1, 8, 36, 37, 77, 80
Gila Cliff Dwellings National Monument 30
Glacier Bay National Park and Preserve 26, 66, 72, 75
Glacier National Park 13, 30, 68, 69, 70, 73, 74, 82, 83
Glen Canyon National Recreation Area 68, 76, 81, 82
Golden Gate National Recreation Area 17, 19, 43, 68, 69, 82
Grand Canyon National Park ii, 22, 67, 68, 70, 74
Grand Canyon-Parashant National Monument 80
Grand Portage National Monument 33, 34, 79
Grand Teton National Park 14, 53, 66, 68, 69, 70, 72, 74
Great Basin National Park 43, 57, 66, 67, 69
Great Sand Dunes National Park and Preserve 30, 57, 66, 67, 68, 69
Great Smoky Mountains National Park 41, 48, 49, 57, 69, 70, 75, 78, 82, 83
Guadalupe Mountains National Park 63
Gulf Islands National Seashore 66, 68, 78

H

Hagerman Fossil Beds National Monument 65
Haleakala National Park 44, 57, 69, 83
Harpers Ferry National Historical Park 36, 64, 77
Hawaii Volcanoes National Park 19, 77
Herbert Hoover National Historic Site 76, 79
Homestead National Monument of America 33, 57, 79
Hopewell Culture National Historical Park 34, 57
Hopewell Furnace National Historic Site 41
Horseshoe Bend National Military Park 65

I

Indiana Dunes National Lakeshore 15, 17, 34, 35, 54, 63, 74
Isle Royale National Park 63, 66, 67, 76

J

Jean Lafitte National Historical Park and Preserve 50, 69, 72, 73, 78, 83

Jewel Cave National Monument 57, 76
John Day Fossil Beds National Monument 44, 57, 69
Johnstown Flood National Memorial 65
Joshua Tree National Park 68

K

Kalaupapa National Historical Park 44, 57, 66
Kaloko-Honokohau National Historical Park 17, 66, 67
Katmai National Park and Preserve 26, 63, 71
Kenai Fjords National Park 27, 28, 73
Kennesaw Mountain National Battlefield Park 65
Kings Mountain National Military Park 80
Klondike Gold Rush National Historical Park 27, 79
Knife River Indian Villages National Historic Site 64
Kobuk Valley National Park 25

L

Lake Clark National Park and Preserve 17, 25, 27, 57, 71, 73
Lake Mead National Recreation Area 30, 66, 68
Lassen Volcanic National Park 44, 65, 68, 69, 83
Lava Beds National Monument 65, 68, 69, 80
Lewis and Clark National Historical Park 16, 54, 80
Little River Canyon National Preserve 50, 57
Lyndon B. Johnson National Historical Park 29, 73

M

Mammoth Cave National Park 14, 50, 72
Manassas National Battlefield Park 37, 64
Mississippi National River and Recreation Area 34
Mojave National Preserve 44, 45, 57, 68, 77
Monocacy National Battlefield 37, 57, 64
Montezuma Castle National Monument 81
Moores Creek National Battlefield 65
Mount Rainier National Park 63, 65, 69, 70
Mount Rushmore National Memorial 79
Muir Woods National Monument 19

N

National Park of American Samoa 18, 80
Natural Bridges National Monument 79
New River Gorge National River 41, 75
Niobrara National Scenic River 34, 83
Noatak National Preserve 25, 69
North Cascades National Park 45, 65, 70, 74

O

Obed Wild and Scenic River 50, 57, 67, 80
Ocmulgee National Monument 65, 80
Olympic National Park 45, 46, 66, 67, 68, 69, 75, 77, 83
Organ Pipe Cactus National Monument 75
Ozark National Scenic Riverways 72, 76, 82

P

Padre Island National Seashore 22, 31, 57, 63, 82, 83
Pecos National Historical Park 31, 79
Petrified Forest National Park 19, 72
Petroglyph National Monument 64
Pictured Rocks National Lakeshore 34, 57, 63
Pinnacles National Monument 75, 82
Pipe Spring National Monument 8, 76, 79
Pipestone National Monument iii, 34, 79
Point Reyes National Seashore 19, 46, 66, 69, 72, 73, 75
Prince William Forest Park 8, 37, 73, 82
Pu'ukohola Heiau National Historic Site 17

R

Redwood National and State Parks 46, 68, 73
Richmond National Battlefield Park 40, 65, 77, 80
Rock Creek Park 38, 57, 76
Rocky Mountain National Park 18, 54, 68, 69, 70, 74, 82, 83
Russell Cave National Monument 50, 70

S

Saguaro National Park 63, 69, 75, 81
Saint Croix National Scenic Riverway 22, 34, 63, 67, 76, 82
Salem Maritime National Historic Site 41
San Antonio Missions National Historical Park 79
Sand Creek Massacre National Historic Site 29
San Francisco Maritime National Historical Park 19
San Juan Island National Historical Park 57, 66
Santa Monica Mountains National Recreation Area 46, 68, 75
Saratoga National Historical Park 15
Saugus Iron Works National Historic Site 41, 57
Sequoia and Kings Canyon National Parks 44, 47, 57, 65, 67, 68, 69, 83

Shenandoah National Park 63, 68, 77
Sitka National Historical Park 64, 79
Sleeping Bear Dunes National Lakeshore 75, 76, 83
Stones River National Battlefield 50, 57, 80
Sunset Crater National Monument 57

T

Theodore Roosevelt National Park 35, 57, 64, 76, 79
Timpanogos Cave National Monument 76, 79
Timucuan Ecological and Historic National Preserve 65
Tumacacori National Monument 76

U

Upper Delaware Scenic and Recreational River 77

V

Valley Forge National Historical Park 40, 77, 80
Valley Forge National Historic Park 63
Vanderbilt Mansion National Historic Site 42
Virgin Islands National Park 51, 57, 83
Voyageurs National Park 70, 74

W

Walnut Canyon National Monument 31, 57
War in the Pacific National Historical Park 14, 80
Washita Battlefield National Historic Site 29
Whiskeytown National Recreation Area 74, 77
White Sands National Monument 67
Wind Cave National Park 67, 68
Wolf Trap National Park for the Performing Arts 38
Wrangell-St. Elias National Park and Preserve 26, 27, 73, 75
Wupatki National Monument 31, 57

Y

Yellowstone National Park 8, 14, 15, 19, 31, 63, 68, 69, 70, 74
Yosemite National Park 44, 47, 65, 68, 69, 70, 83
Yukon-Charley Rivers National Preserve 64, 73

Z

Zion National Park 20, 32, 57, 64, 67, 68

State and Territory Index

A

Alabama 50, 65, 70

Alaska iii, 8, 9, 10, 14, 17, 21, 22, 23, 25, 26, 27, 28, 59, 60, 61, 63, 64, 66, 68, 69, 71, 72, 73, 75, 76, 79, 89

American Samoa 18, 80

Arizona ii, 8, 19, 22, 29, 30, 31, 63, 64, 67, 69, 72, 74, 75, 76, 79, 80, 82

Arkansas 67, 79

C

California 17, 19, 43, 44, 46, 47, 54, 63, 65, 66, 67, 68, 69, 70, 72, 73, 74, 75, 77, 80, 82, 83

Colorado 8, 9, 14, 18, 29, 30, 31, 32, 54, 59, 61, 63, 64, 66, 67, 70, 74, 79, 82, 83

D

District of Columbia 36, 38, 70, 71, 76, 77

F

Florida 1, 9, 15, 18, 19, 22, 48, 49, 51, 53, 54, 59, 61, 65, 66, 67, 68, 70, 71, 75, 78, 83

G

Georgia 39, 49, 54, 65, 67, 73, 78, 80

Guam 14, 43, 80

H

Hawaii 9, 17, 19, 44, 59, 66, 67, 69, 71, 77, 83

I

Idaho 7, 8, 10, 14, 15, 19, 31, 43, 65, 80, 83

Indiana 4, 15, 17, 34, 35, 37, 54, 63, 68, 74, 82

Iowa 76, 79

K

Kentucky 14, 16, 17, 50, 72, 78

L

Louisiana 17, 50, 54, 69, 72, 73, 78, 83

M

Massachusetts 19, 40, 41, 42, 54, 66, 69, 74, 77, 80

Maine 14, 39, 42, 68, 70, 71, 77

Maryland 8, 36, 37, 40, 64, 66, 68, 69, 71, 77, 79, 80

Michigan 34, 63, 66, 67, 75, 76, 83

Minnesota iii, 22, 33, 34, 64, 67, 70, 74, 76, 79, 82

Mississippi 68, 78

Missouri 72, 76, 82

Montana 8, 13, 14, 15, 19, 30, 31, 64, 65, 68, 73, 74, 76, 79, 82, 83

N

North Carolina 22, 41, 48, 49, 54, 65, 67, 69, 70, 75, 78, 80, 82, 83

North Dakota 35, 76, 79

Nebraska 8, 33, 34, 64, 79, 83

Nevada 30, 43, 66, 67

New Jersey 41, 77

New Mexico 14, 30, 31, 57, 63, 64, 67, 69, 75, 79, 82

New York 15, 41, 42, 54, 69, 70, 75, 77

O

Ohio 34, 83

Oklahoma 29, 79

Oregon 16, 44, 45, 54, 65, 70, 80

P

Pennsylvania 39, 40, 41, 63, 65, 77

S

South Carolina 63, 65, 67, 68, 78, 80

South Dakota 22, 33, 64, 67, 68, 74, 75, 76, 79, 83

T

Tennessee 16, 17, 22, 41, 48, 49, 50, 67, 69, 70, 75, 78, 80, 82, 83

Texas 22, 29, 31, 63, 64, 73, 75, 76, 79, 82, 83

U

Utah 14, 20, 28, 29, 32, 63, 64, 67, 76, 79, 82

V

Virginia 1, 8, 17, 37, 38, 40, 42, 48, 63, 64, 65, 66, 68, 69, 71, 73, 77, 78, 80, 82

Virgin Islands 48, 51, 57, 83

W

Washington i, 1, 8, 16, 17, 32, 36, 37, 40, 45, 46, 54, 63, 66, 67, 68, 69, 74, 75, 77, 80, 83, 90

Wisconsin 3, 22, 33, 34, 54, 63, 67, 76, 82

West Virginia 8, 36, 37, 41, 63, 71, 75, 77

Wyoming 8, 14, 15, 19, 31, 53, 63, 64, 66, 69, 72, 74

The Department of the Interior protects and manages the nation's natural resources and cultural heritage; provides scientific and other information about those resources; and honors its special responsibilities to American Indians, Alaska Natives, and affiliated Island Communities.

NPS 909/111147, October 2011

www.ingramcontent.com/pod-product-compliance
Lightning Source LLC
Chambersburg PA
CBHW081831170526
45167CB00007B/2784